The Association Between Base-Area Social and Economic Characteristics and Airmen's Outcomes

Sarah O. Meadows, Laura L. Miller, Jeremy N. V. Miles

RAND Project AIR FORCE

Prepared for the United States Air Force
Approved for public release; distribution unlimited

The research described in this report was sponsored by the United States Air Force under Contract FA7014-06-C-0001. Further information may be obtained from the Strategic Planning Division, Directorate of Plans, Hq USAF.

Library of Congress Control Number: 2014931648

ISBN: 978-0-8330-7859-9

The RAND Corporation is a nonprofit institution that helps improve policy and decisionmaking through research and analysis. RAND's publications do not necessarily reflect the opinions of its research clients and sponsors.

Support RAND—make a tax-deductible charitable contribution at www.rand.org/giving/contribute.html

RAND® is a registered trademark.

Preface

The views expressed are those of the authors and do not reflect the official policy or position of the Department of the Air Force.

A large body of work in sociology and related fields has found that neighborhood characteristics can have an impact on health and well-being beyond individual-level characteristics. Although members of the military and their families move more frequently than the average citizen and, in the case of active-duty service members, have the opportunity to live on a military installation rather than in the general community, the quality and characteristics of the areas where they live can also affect their, and their families', well-being. Military base services in disadvantaged neighborhoods can compensate for the lack of resources needed to be safe, secure, and healthy and to thrive.

Air Force Services asked the RAND Corporation to enhance its ability to tailor support for Airmen and their families through analysis of the relevance of neighborhood, or area, characteristics of the areas surrounding major Air Force installations in the United States. We applied established social indicators and neighborhood studies methodology to (1) score 66 major Air Force installations in terms of their areas' social and economic characteristics and (2) estimate the association between those scores and self-reported Airman outcomes related to health and well-being, military and neighborhood social cohesion, ratings of neighborhood resources, use of on-base resources, satisfaction, and career intentions. The objective was to identify which areas may have greater need for Air Force resources, so that Air Force Services can enhance its programming in those areas and consider this need when making budget decisions. This document reports the results of that analysis. No special expertise is required of readers.

The research reported here was sponsored by the Air Force Office of Airman and Family Services (AF/A1SA) and conducted within the Manpower, Personnel, and Training Program of RAND Project AIR FORCE. It was an update and extension of an earlier RAND-sponsored proof-of-concept study using data from 2000–2003, published in *Exploring the Association Between Military Base Neighborhood Characteristics and Soldiers' and Airmen's Outcomes* by Sarah O. Meadows, Laura L. Miller, Jeremy N. V. Miles, Gabriella C. Gonzalez, and Brandon Dues (TR-1234-RC/A/AF), 2013.

RAND Project AIR FORCE

RAND Project AIR FORCE (PAF), a division of the RAND Corporation, is the U.S. Air Force's federally funded research and development center for studies and analyses.

PAF provides the Air Force with independent analyses of policy alternatives affecting the development, employment, combat readiness, and support of current and future air, space, and cyber forces. Research is conducted in four programs: Force Modernization and Employment; Manpower, Personnel, and Training; Resource Management; and Strategy and Doctrine.

Additional information about PAF is available on our website:
http://www.rand.org/paf

Contents

Figures

Tables

Summary

Military families face many unique stressors, including deployment, separation, threat of harm or injury, and frequent moves. These families rely on a mix of military-provided and community-provided resources to cope with these distinctive stressors. The Air Force requested RAND help enhance its ability to tailor support for Airmen and their families through analysis of the relevance of neighborhood, or area, characteristics of the areas surrounding major Air Force installations in the United States. Building on a prior RAND project (documented in *Exploring the Association Between Military Base Neighborhood Characteristics and Soldiers' and Airmen's Outcomes*, Meadows et al., 2013) and a large literature across multiple academic disciplines that links the qualities and characteristics of neighborhoods to an individual's health and well-being (e.g., sociology, epidemiology, medicine), this study examined whether and how base-area characteristics are associated with individual-level Airman outcomes across several different domains. The objective was to assist the Air Force with identifying communities where Airmen and their families may have greater levels of need so that it can adapt programs or resources to counteract stressors related to the base areas and the lack of nonmilitary resources in the area.

Neighborhood studies among civilians find that the social and economic characteristics of neighborhoods are significant predictors of health and well-being. This literature often focuses on neighborhood advantage or disadvantage, characterized by such factors as socioeconomic status, human capital, degree of personal safety, and availability of recreational activities. Disadvantaged neighborhoods have been empirically linked with worse outcomes, even after accounting for individual factors, such as age, race and ethnicity, gender, and education. This linkage between neighborhood characteristics, or quality, and individual outcomes may occur through multiple mechanisms, but the essential argument is that higher-quality neighborhoods offer residents more resources, better infrastructure, more social interaction, and fewer stressors. Although multiple studies have examined the association between specific neighborhood factors (e.g., unemployment) and retention and satisfaction outcomes among service members and their families, with the exception of one prior RAND report, none has examined the association between general neighborhood or area quality and a range of service member outcomes.

This report addresses three main research questions. First, how much variability is there in the social, economic, and demographic quality of areas surrounding and including Air Force bases? Second, is there an association between these base-area characteristics and Airman outcomes on health and well-being, military and neighborhood social cohesion, ratings of neighborhood resources, use of on-base resources, satisfaction, and career outcomes? If little variability exists or the variability has little influence on Airmen and their families, then a uniform strategy for supporting them across these base areas is justified. If there is variability and an association exists, however, our third question is how the Air Force might use base-area factors in programmatic decisionmaking.

Using data from the U.S. Census Bureau's American Community Survey (2005–2009; U.S. Census Bureau, 2009), we applied standard social indicators methodology to create social and economic profiles of the area encompassed by a 60-minute driving radius around 66 U.S. Air Force installations (including Alaska and Hawaii). Using home ZIP Codes from personnel files, we were able to verify that this definition of *base area* did, in fact, cover areas around the bases where Airmen and their families are concentrated. These area profiles form the basis for the RAND Base Area Social and Economic Index, or the RAND BASE-I. The RAND BASE-I contains 20 indicators of the military and nonmilitary population in these areas, grouped into six domains: household composition, employment, income and poverty, housing, social, and transportation. The RAND BASE-I is not an absolute measure of area quality; rather, it is a way to condense multiple quality indicators into a single index that can be used to compare and contrast characteristics across base areas. The RAND BASE-I should not be interpreted as a list of most-desirable places for Airmen and their families to live. It does not account for other factors that can influence Airman and family preferences for base assignments, such as climate, proximity to family, recreation opportunities, specific employment opportunities for spouses, or preferred Air Force job assignments, such as command or career development opportunities.

RAND BASE-I scores associated with Air Force base areas were quite varied; the gap between the highest-scoring and lowest-scoring areas was large. Geographic clustering among the highest-scoring base areas on the RAND BASE-I was apparent. In general, base areas in the South had lower RAND BASE-I scores, largely due to disadvantages among the economic indicators included in the RAND BASE-I (e.g., family poverty rates and reliance on public assistance among the general population). Yet we caution that the findings do not mean that Airmen and their families are *themselves* in economic distress. Unlike some fellow residents in the general population, for example, active-duty Airmen are employed full time and have housing and health insurance.[1] Thus,

---

[1] Note that, in this report, we refer to both the Active Component and active duty, and to the Reserve Components and reserve status. Reserve and guard members can be on active duty but still be in the Reserve Components; the surveys define those members as being on active duty.

the quality-of-life gap across the general population cannot be taken as an indicator of the quality of life of Airmen. These findings do indicate, however, that some Airmen and their families live in areas where community residents are more financially burdened than residents in other base areas.

After completing the assessment of base-area quality, we applied multilevel modeling techniques to explore possible associations between the RAND BASE-I and its constituent domains and Airman outcomes measured by two different Air Force surveys: the 2011 Community Assessment Survey and the 2010 Caring for People Survey.[2] We grouped the selected Airman outcomes into six different domains: health and well-being, military and neighborhood cohesion, ratings of neighborhood resources, use of on-base resources, satisfaction, and career intentions. We ran separate analyses for active-duty and reserve Airmen, given that reservists are not required to move to a new base assignment every few years and may spend considerable time with civilian employers in other neighborhoods outside of the base. We also tested whether Airmen who live off base and commute to work may be more exposed to social and economic conditions in the larger base area than Airmen who live and work primarily on base. The hypothesis predicts that the association between the RAND BASE-I and Airman outcomes will be stronger among off-base Airmen than on-base Airmen.

At the broadest level of outcomes, we did find significant associations between RAND BASE-I scores and military and neighborhood social cohesion, ratings of neighborhood resources, use of on-base resources, and satisfaction measures. The RAND BASE-I and career outcomes were significantly associated only among reserve Airmen. We did not find that overall base-area quality was associated with the self-reported health and well-being outcomes available on the two Air Force surveys.[3]

For some outcomes, higher scores on the RAND BASE-I aligned well with the interests of the Air Force. For example, among active-duty Airmen, higher scores on the RAND BASE-I are associated with

- greater perceived community safety
- higher satisfaction with community resources
- higher satisfaction with the local base area
- higher satisfaction with access to and the quality of health care
- lower economic stress

---

[2] Both are internal Air Force surveys.

[3] Some associations between the six domains of the RAND BASE-I and Airman outcomes are also significant; these results are presented in appendixes.

- higher perceived school quality
- higher neighborhood quality ratings.

Similarly, among reserve Airmen, higher scores on the RAND BASE-I are associated with

- higher perceived school quality
- higher satisfaction with base assignment
- higher satisfaction with the local base area.

However, for other outcomes, higher RAND BASE-I scores were not aligned with Air Force interests. For example, among active-duty Airmen, higher scores on the RAND BASE-I are associated with

- lower levels of perceived base social cohesion
- lower levels of Airman engagement in the base community
- spending more on child care
- being less likely to use on-base recreational services.

Similarly, among reserve Airmen, higher scores on the RAND BASE-I are associated with

- lower Airman engagement in the base community
- lower perceived neighborhood social cohesion
- using fewer on-base programs and services
- being less likely to use on-base recreational services
- lower satisfaction with quality of own housing
- less perceived support from employers
- lower likelihood of intention to continue or reenlist
- lower likelihood of intention to stay in the Air Force until retirement.

The results suggest that the linkage between neighborhood quality and individual well-being found in civilian studies may be applicable to base-area quality and military populations. For at least some Air Force services, resource allocation at the base level is calculated according to base population sizes. Thus, larger bases receive more resources than smaller bases. However, the Air Force was interested in the social and economic characteristics of base areas because this allocation philosophy does not take into account any variability in base-area stressors and opportunities or what nonmilitary programs, services, and resources may (or may not) be available to Airmen and their families outside the confines of the base. *We find that the RAND BASE-I and indices like it provide one piece of data the Air Force can use to make decisions about service programming and the allocation of limited or scarce resources.* Of course, social and economic indicators of base area are not the *only* data that should be used: Cost, population size, program and service usage rates, and other factors within and outside of

Air Force control should also continue to be taken into account. To illustrate how Air Force Services could apply these base-area findings, we offer five specific examples:

1. **Increase or develop programs to foster a sense of community at higher-scoring bases.** Airmen who live near base areas that ranked higher on the RAND BASE-I reported lower levels of base cohesion. Programs to address this issue would leverage local base leadership, as well as local community leadership, to promote greater interaction and the Wingman Culture.[4]

2. **Focus spouse employment assistance resources in areas with high unemployment.** The existing literature suggests and our research found that Airmen who live near base areas that score high on the overall RAND BASE-I and the employment and income and poverty domains are more satisfied with community job resources. In light of this finding, in locations where area quality is low and unemployment is high, Air Force Services could bolster employment services for Airmen transitioning out of the Air Force, for reservists, and for spouses of current Airmen.

3. **Shift outdoor recreation resources from higher-scoring base areas to lower-scoring ones.** It appears that, in areas that score higher on the RAND BASE-I, Airmen and their families are choosing to utilize off-base, and presumably nonmilitary, resources in their communities when it comes to recreation, especially outdoor recreation. This result suggests that outdoor recreation resources may be more beneficial and better utilized if focused in base areas with fewer resources (those that score lower on the RAND BASE-I).

4. **Consider the RAND BASE-I scores when selecting bases for test programs (e.g., the Food Transformation Initiative).** If a test program does not include both bases located in relatively well-off communities and bases located in poorer communities, the results of the test may be misleading. A test program fielded in a resource-rich community might show limited impact, but, if it had been fielded in a resource-poor community, it might have shown great promise.

5. **Tailor the Air Force Relocation Assistance Program on each base to accentuate where installation resources can compensate for lack of resources in the surrounding community.** We found that Airmen near base areas that ranked higher on the RAND BASE-I reported greater satisfaction with a host of area resources (e.g., child care, jobs, health care). Airmen who live in lower-quality areas may need more information about Air Force programs and services

---

[4] *Wingman Culture* refers to a culture in which Airmen and their families look out for one another and help each other in times of need.

that may bridge the gap between what they need or want and what the outside community can provide.

The RAND BASE-I, or a similar index of neighborhood or base-area quality, may also be useful to the Air Force Medical Service, the Community Action Information Board (CAIB), and the Integrated Delivery System (IDS). Base-area data sources, such as the RAND BASE-I, could be used to identify bases where conditions in the surrounding area may lead to increased stress and strain on Airmen and their families. For example, base areas that score lower on the RAND BASE-I may also result in greater stress among Airmen and family members who live there (e.g., fear of crime and social disorganization may be higher). If this is the case, the Air Force may want to provide additional support for stress-related health care (e.g., counseling services, behavioral health care) to Airmen and their families who live in those areas. Moreover, with an eye to prevention, the Air Force might consider emphasizing resiliency programs for Airmen and their families assigned to bases located in more-stressful environments. The Air Force Medical Service could also use base-area data to identify areas where out-of-network, civilian providers may be more plentiful and augment existing resources with services from the area. CAIBs and IDSs (Air Force level, major command [MAJCOM] level, and base level) might also find information about the relative resources of base areas helpful in their efforts to foster collaborative partnerships with service providers and helping agencies in the community.

Installation commanders can also use neighborhood or base-area quality data. Our results suggest that commanders whose installations are located in areas where the RAND BASE-I score of the base area is high may suffer from lower perceived base cohesion. This suggests a tension between a highly cohesive base environment and a civilian area around the base that scores high on our measure of quality. The finding suggests that base commanders in those areas that score higher on the RAND BASE-I may need to make extra efforts to foster base cohesion and sense of community among Airmen assigned to their bases, especially those who live off base. Commanders can also use the RAND BASE-I, or similar indices, to take stock of the local community. A specialized index would allow them to focus on issues most relevant to the Airmen directly under their command and those Airmen's families. Such indices may also be helpful in change-of-command situations and provide incoming commanders a quick lay of the land.

Finally, we assert that military researchers can also use neighborhood and area quality to inform their studies. Some existing and ongoing data sets frequently used by military researchers, both military and civilian, could easily be linked to geographically based data, such as the census. Examples include the surveys used in this study (i.e., the Community Assessment Survey and the Caring for People Survey), the Defense

Manpower Data Center's Status of Forces Survey, and the U.S. Department of Defense's (DoD's) Millennium Cohort Study. The addition of this type of data can expand the explanatory power of analyses. Ultimately, understanding how and why the social and economic characteristics of geographic areas may affect the health and well-being of service members and their families, their satisfaction with military life, and their retention and career decisions can be an additional consideration in how policymakers and military leadership design and implement policies affecting military members and their families.

Acknowledgments

We would like to thank Eliza Nesmith and Karen Terry from Airman and Family Readiness in the Air Force Services office, who sponsored this project because they were seeking ways to better understand the communities in which Airmen and their families live. They provided feedback on the initial social indicators portion of the study and facilitated access to the Community Assessment Survey. After Tamre Newton joined Air Force Services in 2012, she took over as project monitor for the last portion of the study. We also thank Curt Cornelssen, who facilitated access to the Caring for People Survey and provided the context of Air Force base transformation efforts while he was chief of the Air Force Services' Future Operations office. Cornelssen's successor in 2012, Lt. Col. Christopher Lavallee, worked with us during the latter half of the project to help us think about how this study could inform Air Force base transformation plans. This report also benefited from conversations about the relevance of this study to the Air Force held with Horace L. Larry, Deputy Director of Air Force Services, Deputy Chief of Staff for Manpower and Personnel, Headquarters U.S. Air Force; Tamre Newton; Col. Jay Stone, Deputy Director of Psychological Health and chair of the Air Force Integrated Delivery System; and Carl Buchanan, executive director of the Air Force Community Action Information Board.

This study would not have been possible without the support of our RAND colleagues Lisa Miyashiro, who helped map where Airmen live using Air Force personnel data and mapping software; Martha Timmer, who helped with census data collection and constructing the main index of area quality; and Aaron Kofner, who helped to define 30-, 60-, and 90-minute driving radii around the 66 installations included in our study. We also thank Hosay Salam Yaqub and Donna White, who assisted us with preparing this manuscript for publication. Brian Gifford of the Integrated Benefits Institute and Terry Schell from RAND contributed to the development of this report through their careful and constructive reviews of an earlier version of this manuscript. We also appreciate the many hours Lisa Bernard spent editing this document, with all of its challenging tables and figures. Kimbria McCarty's management of the editing process was also key to the preparation of the final report.

Abbreviations

ACC	Air Combatant Command
ACS	American Community Survey
AETC	Air Education and Training Command
AF/A1SA	Air Force Office of Airman and Family Services
AFB	Air Force base
AFGSC	Air Force Global Strike Command
AFMC	Air Force Materiel Command
AFSOC	Air Force Special Operations Command
AFSPC	Air Force Space Command
AMC	Air Mobility Command
BAH	basic allowance for housing
CAIB	Community Action Information Board
CD-RISC	Connor-Davidson Resilience Scale
CES-D	Center for Epidemiologic Studies Depression Scale
CONUS	continental United States
CWI	Child and Youth Well-Being Index
DoD	U.S. Department of Defense
EFMP	Exceptional Family Member Program
FTI	Food Transformation Initiative
FY	fiscal year
HPSA	Health Professional Shortage Area
HRSA	Health Resources and Services Administration
IDS	Integrated Delivery System
JB	joint base
MAJCOM	major command
MSA	metropolitan statistical area
NAF	naval air facility
NCO	noncommissioned officer
OD	origin–destination
PACAF	Pacific Air Forces
PAF	RAND Project AIR FORCE
PCS	permanent change of station
QOL	quality of life

RAND BASE-I	RAND Base Area Social and Economic Index that averages each of the six domain scores
RAND BASE-I(I)	RAND Base Area Social and Economic Index that weights each of the 20 indicators equally, without calculating any domain scores
RAND BASE-I(Z)	RAND Base Area Social and Economic Index that uses a z-score transformation to constrain variances of the indicators
SD	standard deviation
SES	socioeconomic status
SNIAC	Special Needs Identification Assignment Coordination
UA	urban area
UC	urban cluster

Chapter One. Associations Between Neighborhood Social and Economic Characteristics and Resident Health and Well-Being

Airmen and their families live under many stresses—frequent moves, deployments, reintegration following deployments—and rely on the Air Force for resources to help safeguard the health and well-being of themselves and their families. Many of these resources are utilized at the base level. That is, each Air Force base (AFB) has a set of offices, programs, and individuals whose responsibilities include providing information, education, health care, recreational programs and facilities, and other programs and services to enhance the quality of life (QOL) and organizational commitment of Airmen and their families. But Airmen and their families may also rely on resources available in the communities surrounding the installation to which they are assigned or, if they commute to the base, in the neighborhoods and base areas where they live.

Active-duty Airmen and their families are typically reassigned to a different base every few years. With each move, military families must find new housing, new schools, new places to exercise or socialize, and, for many spouses, a new job. Families may need to adapt to new climates, security environments, regional cultures and customs, neighbors, co-workers and supervisors, and more. Just as not all bases are the same, not all families who are assigned to those bases are the same. The area surrounding a base and, more importantly, the resources it provides also vary. The relative quality of bases and their surrounding areas can have an important influence on Airmen's and families' social support networks, job and life satisfaction, and overall health and well-being. Reserve Airmen are not required to move from base to base and thus may have more control over where they live, and particularly over what neighborhood they choose. Because frequent moves are not required, they may have greater residential stability than active-duty Airmen and thus greater exposure to neighborhood and base-area characteristics, such as poverty, crime rates, social support networks.

This report considers the possible impact that base-area social and economic climates can have on Airmen and their families; a large and growing body of research has found an association between neighborhood characteristics and individual-level health and well-being (Diez Roux and Mair, 2010; Kawachi and Berkman, 2003; Renalds, Smith, and Hale, 2010). If the social and economic characteristics of base areas do have an impact on Airmen and their families, and quality of those characteristics varies across bases, then how can the Air Force most effectively and efficiently meet the varying needs of its members, especially in a period in which budgets are being slashed? The current model of resource allocation based on base population size may have undesirable unintended consequences, particularly at bases located in the poorest communities. For this reason, Air Force Services was interested in learning more about the potential impact of base-area characteristics and how it could counteract negative factors and leverage the positive ones. We assert that a more nuanced approach is warranted when the geographic areas containing AFBs vary in terms of their ability to support the needs of Airmen and their families.[5]

How Neighborhoods Could Influence Health and Well-Being

Three mechanisms have been implicated in the link between neighborhood characteristics and individual health and well-being. The first is collective efficacy, sometimes called *social capital* or *social cohesion* (see Coleman, 1988; Sampson, 2003, Putnam, 1996). These terms refer to various aspects of a neighborhood's ability to create a sense of community or togetherness among residents. They reflect the strength of social connections in a neighborhood. Neighborhoods high in collective efficacy are characterized as places where individuals know each other, where they have the capacity to reach collective goals, where people trust each other, and where informal social control can regulate behavior. Such high-quality neighborhoods not only can directly influence positive health behaviors through informal social control but also can promote psychological well-being through perceptions of social support and trust (Sampson, 2003).

The second linking mechanism is the quality of the neighborhood's infrastructure or resources. This includes abandoned buildings, broken windows, graffiti, access to parks and recreation, and pollution and air quality. The key aspect of this mechanism is the physical environment of the neighborhood. It is important to note that this mechanism can be either negative or positive, depending on the physical environment to which residents are exposed. Raudenbush (2003) found that exposure to social disorder—such things as abandoned cars and buildings, defaced property, garbage, drug paraphernalia, and public prostitution—are associated with worse physical health outcomes. However, other research has linked accessibility to parks and other green spaces to greater usage of such areas and ultimately to residents' physical and mental health (Lee and Maheswaran, 2010). Regardless of whether the physical environment is positive or negative, the key to

---

[5] An earlier RAND proof-of-concept study addressed the variability and potential impact of base neighborhoods on Airmen using census and Air Force data from 2000 to 2003 (see Meadows et al., 2013).

this mechanism is the availability of resources (or lack thereof) necessary to promote community health and well-being.

The third linking mechanism is stress. Individuals who live in low-quality neighborhoods, which may be characterized by high crime rates and other signs of neighborhood disorganization, or social disorder (e.g., graffiti, broken windows), few areas for safe recreational activity, and little access to healthy food options, internalize the stress of living in such environments. This experience of stress affects physical health and well-being through physiological responses that mimic the body's "fight-or-flight" response, which is characterized by an increase in the release of certain hormones (e.g., adrenaline, noradrenaline, epinephrine, cortisol). Extended exposure to stress can result in the breakdown of important physiological processes, which, in turn, can have deleterious effects on cardiovascular, metabolic, immune, brain activity, or central nervous system functioning (McEwen, 1998). Some studies have found that health disparities across individuals in different neighborhoods can be attributed to differential stress levels experienced by area residents (Boardman, 2004; Matthews and Yang, 2010).

Outcomes Linked to Neighborhoods

Existing neighborhood research focuses primarily on health and well-being outcomes. In our previous exploration of the association between military base neighborhood characteristics and service member outcomes, we reviewed the literature and provided numerous examples of this research (see Table 2.2 in Meadows et al., 2013, for references). Common outcome measures include infectious diseases (e.g., sexually transmitted infections), chronic diseases (e.g., cardiovascular disease, diabetes, asthma), adult mortality, infant mortality, low birth weight, and infant health, health risk behaviors (e.g., smoking, drug and alcohol abuse), obesity, mental health (e.g., suicidal behavior, depression), and self-rated health.

Noticeably absent from this literature are studies that link subjective ratings of one's neighborhood to more-objective neighborhood quality indicators. For example, self-rated satisfaction with one's neighborhood, or perceptions of neighborhood cohesiveness and safety, may also be correlated with objective measures of neighborhood status (e.g., unemployment rates, education rates). In some sense, a high correlation between the two (i.e., subjective and objective measures) will validate that an index of neighborhood characteristics does, in fact, tap into a latent measure of quality. And, from the perspective of the Air Force, it may be important to know whether the use of services by Airmen and their families varies according to the quality of the neighborhoods. If use of on-base, Air Force–sponsored programs and facilities are indeed higher in lower-quality neighborhoods, then a disproportionate distribution of resources to those programs can be justified as compensatory for the lack of quality programs or facilities in the community and meeting the needs of Airmen and their families. Thus, our analysis will include both more-traditional measures of Airman health and well-being and measures of community satisfaction and service utilization.

Qualities and Characteristics of Neighborhoods Linked to Outcomes

As noted in the previous section, certain aspects or characteristics of neighborhoods have been implicated in the neighborhood–health link. Two general types of indicators are available: objective and subjective (see Weden, Carpiano, and Robert, 2008). Most often, objective measures of neighborhood characteristics are related to the overall socioeconomic status (SES) of the area. These indicators include such measures as median income, poverty rates, and unemployment rates and are typically obtained from large demographic data sets, such as the census. Researchers tend to view this type of data as indicators of neighborhood *disadvantage* (Ross and Mirowsky, 2001, 2009), although some common measures, such as the percentage of residents with a college degree, tap neighborhood *affluence*, rather than disadvantage (Johnson, 2008; Massey, 1996).

A second set of objective neighborhood characteristics is those associated with researcher or observer assessments of a neighborhood's general QOL. These include such things as crime and other measures of social disorganization (e.g., broken windows, abandoned buildings, graffiti) (see Raudenbush and Sampson, 1999; Sampson and Raudenbush, 2004) and the built environment (e.g., land-use mix, walkability, residential density) (see Sallis et al., 2009).

Because objective measures of neighborhood characteristics may not capture the experiences of residents, some research has used subjective measures of neighborhood quality (see Echeverria, Diez-Roux, and Link, 2004; Ross and Mirowsky, 2001, 2009; Schaefer-McDaniel, 2009). Such measures can include perceptions of safety, pollution, and social cohesion. The key to subjective measures is that they are obtained from residents themselves and not from administrative or census data. As such, the assumption is that subjective data more accurately convey the aspects of a neighborhood that are most salient for health and well-being (Cummins et al., 2007).

Both quantitative and qualitative metrics of neighborhood quality have been linked to health and well-being (see Cummins et al., 2007; Diez Roux, 2001; and Macintyre, Ellaway, and Cummins, 2002). However, fewer studies have simultaneously measured both types of measures to assess their differential impact. Weden, Carpiano, and Robert (2008) find that both do matter for health, specifically for depressive symptoms and self-rated health (net of other individual-level characteristics). But important to note is that, in that study, perceived neighborhood quality (i.e., the subjective measure) was more strongly associated with health outcomes than were objective measures of neighborhood disadvantage and affluence. Further, subjective perceptions of neighborhood quality mediated the association between objective measures of neighborhood quality and health. That is, objective characteristics of a neighborhood (e.g., poverty, use of public assistance, education level, unemployment) were associated with individuals' perceptions of their neighborhoods, which, in turn, were associated with health (see also J. Kim, 2010). Unfortunately, as we note in the next section, the availability of subjective measures of neighborhoods and their characteristics is sometimes problematic.

Challenges to Applying Neighborhood Studies

Although the field of neighborhood studies has gained much ground in the past three decades, there are still challenges that have yet to be completely addressed. First, short of randomly assigning individuals to neighborhoods, we cannot definitely assert that neighborhood characteristics *cause* any given outcome at the individual level (for example, see McCormack and Shiell, 2011). Because individuals can and do select where they live, it is possible that other factors (e.g., wealth) are responsible for individual health and well-being outcomes, as well as residence (and, therefore, the characteristics of that residence). SES is a particularly difficult factor to rule out because neighborhoods are generally stratified by SES, and SES affects health (Diez Roux, 2001). Military populations are a unique case in which choice of neighborhood is constrained because service members are assigned to bases, although many have the ability to choose whether to live on or off base and, if off base, in which exact neighborhood they want to live. Those choices may be shaped by such factors as affordability of housing, school quality, crime rates, recommendations from their social networks or relocation or housing assistance programs, and whether service members have the opportunity to visit neighborhoods in person before deciding or whether they search solely from afar through the Internet.

Second, the definition of a neighborhood is not stable across time, individuals, or research question. *Neighborhood* can mean different things to different people. A recent qualitative study of adolescents and their parents found four factors that individuals use to define their own neighborhoods: physical and institutional characteristics (e.g., roads, parks, schools), sociodemographic characteristics (e.g., race or ethnicity, class of residents), perceived criminal threats both within and outside, and symbolic identities (e.g., shared values or history) (Campbell et al., 2009). These factors represent an individual's *subjective* identification of his or her neighborhood. Objectively, we can also measure an individual's neighborhood by using a standard geographic dimension—a census block or tract, a ZIP Code, or a city boundary. To complicate matters even further, these "standard" geographic dimensions can shift over time. New ZIP Codes are sometimes created, for example. Ultimately, the research question that is being addressed may drive the decision of how to define *neighborhood*. If one is interested in neighborhood effects on teen smoking, it may be useful to define neighborhoods based on where teens spend their leisure time. But if one is interested in how the walkability of a neighborhood influences population-level obesity, it may be more useful to use a definition of *neighborhood* that ties closely with existing geographic boundaries.

The decision of how to measure neighborhood is closely tied with a third challenge of neighborhood research: where to get neighborhood data. If one uses individual-level, subjective definitions of neighborhoods, then census-tract data may be of little use because of the wide variability in how well they would match subjective definitions. However, if one needs data that can be consistently compared across specific geographies, or that are considered comparable across a large geography (e.g., across the entire United States), then standardized data may be more appropriate. In general, area data can come from individual perceptions, researcher observations, or official sources, such as the census or state or local governments. Some data can be obtained from for-profit or nongovernmental organizations, such as the National Association of Realtors, but often these data are proprietary, must be purchased, or cannot easily be matched to other geographic units of analysis.

A fourth challenge associated with neighborhood studies is how to combine multiple facets of neighborhoods. If one is interested in only one aspect of a neighborhood—say, the average SES—existing modeling techniques can easily accommodate such an analysis. But if the goal is to characterize neighborhood across multiple dimensions, across a set of different indicators, then we need a way to simply and efficiently, without sacrificing information, combine those neighborhood characteristics in a meaningful way. One mechanism for doing so is to use social indicators methodology to create a composite index of neighborhood characteristics.

Social Indicators Research and Composite Indices

Because a single model of health and well-being with dozens of neighborhood characteristics entered as predictors is unwieldy, it is necessary to use some method to combine those characteristics into one data point that is comparable across multiple neighborhoods. This is exactly what a composite index does. Social indicators methodology, which frequently makes use of such indices, is often used to compare or rank-order geographic units, such as nations, states, or cities, as well as groups of people (e.g., citizens of a country, children).

Social indicators research has a long history in the United States (Cobb and Rixford, 1998) and has been used to influence social policy. If we consider solely QOL studies, we see that policymakers have become increasingly reliant on composite indices to gauge the health and well-being of populations since the late 1990s (Land, 2000; Lippman, 2007) and, subsequently, to recommend policies that are aimed at areas where health and well-being have declined or are lower than some set standard. QOL indices make it relatively easy to combine multiple indicators yet, at the same time, allow for disaggregation of indicators when necessary. For example, one QOL index may combine measures of health among both adults and children. When child-only policies are of interest, policymakers can focus specifically on those indicators relevant to the subpopulation of interest. Such indices also make it easy to compare QOL over time, making them a sort of social barometer. Examples include the Index of Social Health (Miringoff and Miringoff, 1999), which uses 16 measures of social, economic, and health well-being to assess overall well-being among Americans, and the Child and Youth Well-Being Index (CWI) (Land, Lamb, and Mustillo, 2001), which similarly focuses on health and well-being but only of children and youths, by tracking some 25 national-level indicators.

The Relevance of Military Base Areas

Previous research has considered the role that on-base services and base-area neighborhood characteristics may play in the QOL and level of commitment to military service for military personnel and their spouses. For example, such resources as libraries, child and youth programs, child-care programs, fitness centers, and campgrounds, have been associated with satisfaction with military life (Booth, Segal, and Bell, 2007; Nord, Perry, and Maxfield, 1997; Westhuis and Fafara, 2007). Research has also explored how neighborhood school quality influences the housing choices of military personnel (Wenger and Hodari, 2002), how characteristics of job markets around military bases affect the employment of military spouses (Harrell et al., 2004; Hosek et al., 2002), and how child-care characteristics matter both for spouse satisfaction and for the performance of military personnel (MacDermid et al., 2008; Zellman et al., 2009). Research has considered the impact that military bases can have on the surrounding community as well, such as the influence on local labor markets (Booth, 2003) and on local health care safety nets (Gifford, 2005).

However, with the exception of an exploratory study conducted by the authors of this report (Meadows et al., 2013), social indicators methodology has not been used to convey, in a greatly condensed fashion, the types of information that could help the armed services understand variation across their installations and the role that the social and economic factors might play in the health and well-being, QOL, or career commitment of their families and service members.

The Current Study

One important difference between the current study and existing neighborhood studies literature should be noted at the outset. The definition of *neighborhood* used in this study is generally much larger than that used in the existing literature (see Chapter Two for details). *Neighborhood*, in this case, is linked to employment (or base assignment), which is rarely the case in other studies. For these reasons, and to avoid confusion, we use the term *base area* rather than *base neighborhood*. Nonetheless, we still use similar concepts and methods from existing neighborhood studies.

The current study asks three primary research questions:

- How much variability is there in the social, economic, and demographic qualities of AFB areas?
- Is there an association between these area characteristics and Airman outcomes on
    - perceived health and well-being
    - perceived military and neighborhood social cohesion
    - ratings of neighborhood resources
    - use of on-base resources
    - satisfaction
    - career intentions?
- If an association exists, how might the Air Force use area factors in decisionmaking?

The main goal of this study was to provide the Air Force with data that may help it to determine how to more efficiently, and effectively, provide services, resources, and leadership to address the needs of its population by providing a composite look at base-area characteristics and how those characteristics may influence individual outcomes. Such a goal requires the use of a standard methodology not only to score bases and their surrounding areas but also to assess whether or not those scores are associated with self-reported measures of Airman outcomes.

Although providing the Air Force with one possible rational for more-efficient, effective service provision was the main goal of the study, it is important to note that, in some ways, this goal is a means to an end. Ultimately, the Air Force is interested in many things that may relate to support services and programs. For example, appropriate mental and behavioral health care services may lead to fewer behavioral and health problems among Airmen and their families. If Airmen and their families are satisfied with the services and programs provided to them, then overall satisfaction with the Air Force may also be high, and thus retention may be (positively) affected.

We offer Figure 1.1 as a backdrop against which to understand the context of this study. The model of neighborhood or area influence on Airmen and their family members is drawn primarily from the civilian literature (reviewed above). On the left of the figure are neighborhood and area quality: social, economic, and demographic. Those characteristics are then associated with an Airman's stress levels, how integrated he or she perceives him- or herself to be both into the neighborhood or area itself and within the base or installation, how satisfied he or she is across multiple dimensions (e.g., life, the Air Force, the civilian area), and the extent to which he or she reports using services both on and off base. Although these factors could be considered outcomes in and of themselves, they can also be viewed as intermediary steps between neighborhood or area characteristics and quality and other more-distal outcomes important to the Air Force. These more-distal outcomes include such things as mental and physical health, general well-being, and retention. Our analysis will focus on both proximate outcomes (i.e., the center arrow) and more-distal outcomes (i.e., the last arrow).

Figure 1.1
Model of Neighborhood and Area Characteristics and Airman and Family Outcomes

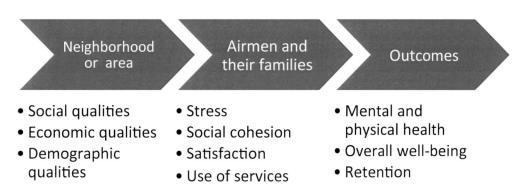

In the next chapter, we provide more detail on the data and methods used in the analysis. Chapter Three presents results from the RAND Base Area Social and Economic Index (RAND BASE-I), which uses a social indicators approach to score base areas. Chapters Four and Five offer key findings from the multilevel models linking the RAND BASE-I to Airman responses to selected items on the Community Assessment Survey and the Caring for People Survey, respectively. These items correspond to the proximate and distal outcomes in Figure 1.1. And finally, Chapter Six summarizes the research and proposes policy implications based on the findings reported in earlier chapters.

Chapter Two. Data and Methodology

This chapter describes the data and methods used in this study. It first describes how we selected Air Force installations included in the analysis and defined base areas. The chapter also details the data and methods used to create the RAND BASE-I. Finally, the chapter provides a brief description of the survey data used for the analyses described in the subsequent two chapters about the association between RAND BASE-I scores and Airman outcomes. Because this chapter focuses on data sources and methods, readers interested in skipping to the study results may wish to skip to Chapter Three.

Selecting Installations and Defining the Base-Area Boundaries

We limited the sample of Air Force installations to those located in the United States (including Alaska and Hawaii), given the lack of international neighborhood-level data that would be comparable to U.S. data. In order to ensure that our later statistical modeling strategy would be supported, we also limited our sample of installations to those with at least 1,000 full-time permanent party military personnel. This excluded temporary visitors to military installations, such as patients, trainees, and students who did not make a permanent change of station (PCS) to a schoolhouse. Applying these criteria, we selected our sample using information on installation location and population size in the *USAF Almanac* for 2010 (U.S. Air Force, 2010), which extended our analysis to 66 Air Force installations, listed in Table 2.1.[6] Note that some installations on the list are not owned by the Air Force, as is the case with the Pentagon, Pope Field, Fort George Meade, and the joint bases (JBs) shared with other services. We include these installations because of the large presence of Airmen assigned there.

---

[6] As a general rule, the multilevel modeling technique we utilized requires that a minimum of 30 aggregated units or, in this case, installations be included to accurately estimate model parameters and have sufficient power to detect significant effects. Our sample size met this criterion.

Table 2.1
List of 66 Installations Used in the Base-Area Analysis

Altus AFB, OK	Goodfellow AFB, TX	Nellis AFB, NV
JB Anacostia-Bolling, DC	Grand Forks AFB, ND	Offutt AFB, NE
JB Andrews-NAF Washington, MD	Hanscom AFB, MA	Patrick AFB, FL
Arnold AFB, TN	Hill AFB, UT	JB Pearl Harbor–Hickam, HI
Barksdale AFB, LA	Holloman AFB, NM	Pentagon, VA
Beale AFB, CA	Hurlburt Field, FL	Peterson AFB, CO
Buckley AFB, CO	Keesler AFB, MS	Pope Field, NC
Cannon AFB, NM	Kirtland AFB, NM	Robins AFB, GA
JB Charleston, SC	JB Langley-Eustis, VA	JB San Antonio, TX
Columbus AFB, MS	Laughlin AFB, TX	Schriever AFB, CO
Creech AFB, NV	JB Lewis-McChord, WA	Scott AFB, IL
Davis-Monthan AFB, AZ	Little Rock AFB, AR	Seymour Johnson AFB, NC
Dover AFB, DE	Los Angeles AFB, CA	Shaw AFB, SC
Dyess AFB, TX	Luke AFB, AZ	Sheppard AFB, TX
Edwards AFB, CA	MacDill AFB, FL	Tinker AFB, OK
Eglin AFB, FL	Malmstrom AFB, MT	Travis AFB, CA
Eielson AFB, AK	Maxwell AFB, AL	Tyndall AFB, FL
Ellsworth AFB, SD	McConnell AFB, KS	U.S. Air Force Academy, CO
JB Elmendorf-Richardson, AK	JB McGuire-Dix-Lakehurst, NJ	Vance AFB, OK
Fairchild AFB, WA	Minot AFB, ND	Vandenberg AFB, CA
F. E. Warren AFB, WY	Moody AFB, GA	Whiteman AFB, MO
Fort George G. Meade, MD	Mountain Home AFB, ID	Wright-Patterson AFB, OH

NOTE: NAF = naval air facility.

As we have previously noted, existing neighborhood studies use a variety of means to define neighborhoods. Our challenge was to define base neighborhoods, or areas, in a way that would capture not only the geographic area of the base itself but also areas where Airmen and their families tend to live and may spend a significant portion of their time. Neighborhoods or areas defined too narrowly (e.g., just the base itself) would exclude many areas where Airmen and their families live, work, shop, participate in recreational activities, and use other types of resources. Neighborhoods or areas defined too broadly run the risk of masking any impact of the areas most relevant for most service members and their families.

Using data from Air Force personnel files and mapping software, we mapped Airmen's permanent addresses by ZIP Code.[7] Figure 2.1 shows the distribution of all Active Component and Reserve Component Airmen by ZIP Code across the United States. The 66 installations included in our analysis are also noted on the map. Comparable maps that display Active Component Airmen separately from Reserve Component Airmen can be found in Appendix A. Darker shades of purple indicate a higher concentration of Airmen within the same ZIP Code; white areas reflect regions where no Airman residences were indicated. Given that Airmen are not uniformly concentrated in concentric rings around each base, we examined each installation to identify an optimal base-area definition.

---

[7] One limitation of using the permanent address of Airmen from personnel files is that the information may not reflect where Airmen live. For example, we found instances in which Airmen who were assigned to one base listed a permanent address several states away. Because service members can have permanent addresses for residency and tax purposes independent of the homes they establish near their base assignments, not all of this information reflects the addresses where Airmen are actually living. Ideally, both permanent addresses and current residences would be available in the personnel files. Although these data are imperfect, for our purposes, they do indicate where Airmen tend to cluster around bases. All of the mapping and geospatial processing were performed using ESRI's ArcMap suite of mapping software.

Figure 2.1

Distribution of Active Component and Reserve Component Air Force Personnel, by ZIP Code

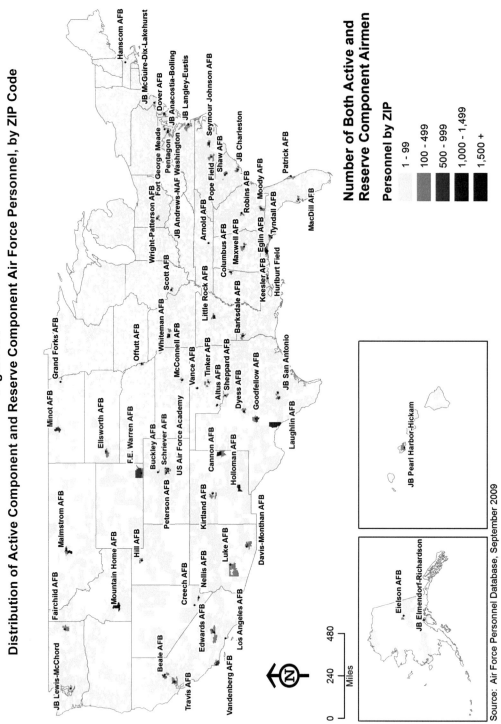

Number of Both Active and Reserve Component Airmen

Personnel by ZIP

1 - 99
100 - 499
500 - 999
1,000 - 1,499
1,500 +

Source: Air Force Personnel Database, September 2009

NOTE: The figure shows only installations with more than 1,000 permanent party Airmen.

Figure 2.2 provides a base-specific example of the mapping procedure we performed for each base before determining the base-area definition appropriate for this study. This example focuses on Grand Forks AFB in North Dakota. The figure shows a shading pattern reflecting the concentration of Airmen that is similar to that in Figure 2.1. In the figure, the yellow line around the base indicates a 30-minute (not 30-mile) driving radius.[8] Notice that this boundary misses many of the purple-shaded ZIP Codes where Airmen live. A 60-minute driving radius, bounded by the green line, does capture a larger proportion of the purple ZIP Codes. The final boundary, the red line, shows a 90-minute radius around Grand Forks AFB. Although this boundary does capture the bulk of the Airman population at the base, it begins to capture more ZIP Codes where Airmen do not live than ZIP Codes where Airmen do.

_____

[8] In order to calculate the driving radii, ArcMap's Network Analyst extension was used. For all network analyses, a North American street map file was used as the underlying spatial network. A service area was calculated for each AFB centroid at 30-, 60-, and 90-minute cutoff times. Driving radii do not take traffic into account. They rely on posted speed limits on existing roads and highways. To calculate whether a census tract was within a given distance of an AFB, an origin–destination (OD) matrix was calculated between base centroids and tract centroids. Only those OD pairs contained within the specified driving radii were included in subsequent analyses of a base's area characteristics.

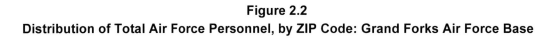

Figure 2.2
Distribution of Total Air Force Personnel, by ZIP Code: Grand Forks Air Force Base

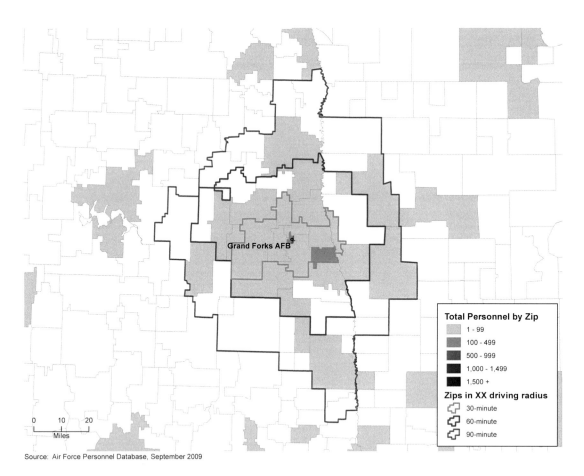

Source: Air Force Personnel Database, September 2009

As seen in Figures 2.3, 2.4, and 2.5, for some installations, such as Luke AFB, F. E. Warren AFB, and JB San Antonio, the 30-minute boundary misses a significant portion of Airmen living near the base. At the same time, increasing the boundary from 60 to 90 minutes results in an increasing number of areas where there are no Airmen present (see Figures 2.2 and 2.3, especially).

Figure 2.3
Distribution of Total Air Force Personnel, by ZIP Code: Luke Air Force Base

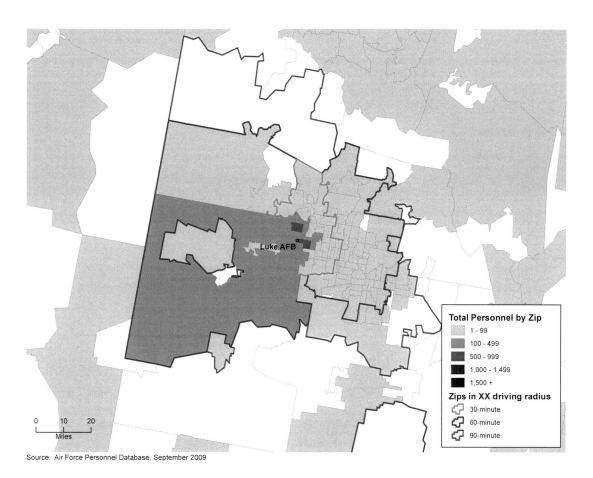

Source: Air Force Personnel Database, September 2009

17

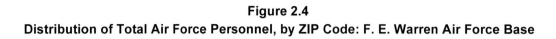

Figure 2.4
Distribution of Total Air Force Personnel, by ZIP Code: F. E. Warren Air Force Base

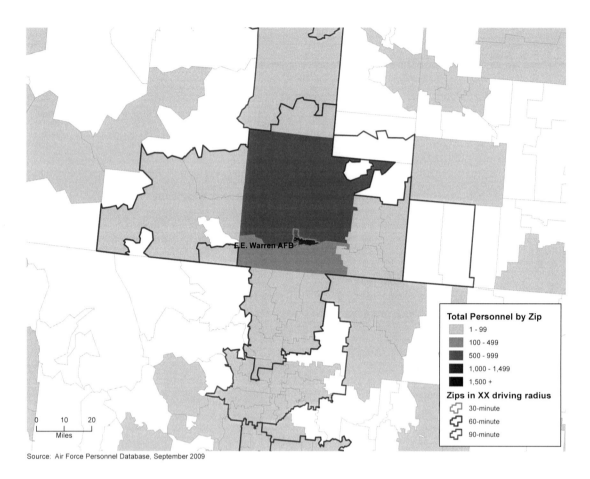

Source: Air Force Personnel Database, September 2009

18

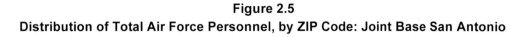

Figure 2.5
Distribution of Total Air Force Personnel, by ZIP Code: Joint Base San Antonio

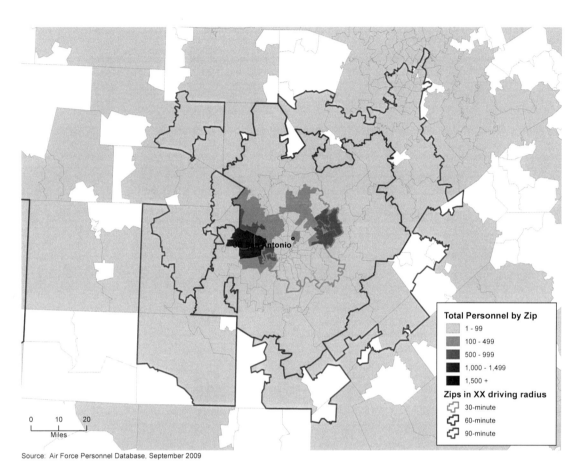

Source: Air Force Personnel Database, September 2009

According to careful examination of the density maps, driving radii for each of the 66 installations in our analysis, and consultation with Air Force Services, the office that sponsored this research, we decided to define the base area for our study as the ZIP Code where the base is located plus those that fall into the 60-minute driving radius.[9]

It is important to note that our construction of base areas differs significantly in size from the neighborhoods used in much of the existing neighborhood studies literature. For example, according to Table 2.2, the square mileage encompassed by some base areas can be as large as 10,000, as is the case for F. E. Warren and Mountain Home AFBs. These bases are generally in rural areas where population density is quite low. In contrast, many existing neighborhood studies use construction of neighborhoods (or geographic areas) that are much smaller—city blocks, towns, or even the street where a respondent

---

[9] RAND BASE-I results using both the 30- and 90-minute boundaries are presented in Appendix B.

lives. Ultimately, there is no right or wrong way to construct a base area. We simply point out that there are alternatives to the methods we used.

Table 2.2
Square Mileage of 66 Base Areas

Base Area	Square Miles	Base Area	Square Miles
Altus AFB, OK	2,085	Little Rock AFB, AR	2,990
JB Anacostia-Bolling, DC	1,646	Los Angeles AFB, CA	222
JB Andrews-NAF Washington, MD	2,176	Luke AFB, AZ	6,886
Arnold AFB, TN	299	MacDill AFB, FL	1,597
Barksdale AFB, LA	3,801	Malmstrom AFB, MT	3,724
Beale AFB, CA	3,572	Maxwell AFB, AL	3,223
Buckley AFB, CO	4,226	McConnell AFB, KS	3,509
Cannon AFB, NM	5,188	JB McGuire-Dix-Lakehurst, NJ	1,320
JB Charleston, SC	2,721	Minot AFB, ND	5,194
Columbus AFB, MS	2,658	Moody AFB, GA	1,740
Creech AFB, NV	3,134	Mountain Home AFB, ID	10,352
Davis-Monthan AFB, AZ	3,825	Nellis AFB, NV	3,416
Dover AFB, DE	1,726	Offutt AFB, NE	3,386
Dyess AFB, TX	3,525	Patrick AFB, FL	1,605
Edwards AFB, CA	4,111	JB Pearl Harbor–Hickam, HI	584
Eglin AFB, FL	1,752	Pentagon, VA	2,210
Eielson AFB, AK	7,274	Peterson AFB, CO	3,210
Ellsworth AFB, SD	7,647	Pope Field, NC	2,163
JB Elmendorf-Richardson, AK	5,848	Robins AFB, GA	2,200
Fairchild AFB, WA	4,228	JB San Antonio, TX	3,348
F. E. Warren AFB, WY	10,816	Schriever AFB, CO	2,302
Fort George G. Meade, MD	1,142	Scott AFB, IL	3,037
Goodfellow AFB, TX	1,767	Seymour Johnson AFB, NC	2,355
Grand Forks AFB, ND	3,906	Shaw AFB, SC	1,932
Hanscom AFB, MA	1,204	Sheppard AFB, TX	3,183
Hill AFB, UT	9,561	Tinker AFB, OK	3,440
Holloman AFB, NM	6,785	Travis AFB, CA	2,618
Hurlburt Field, FL	1,530	Tyndall AFB, FL	1,592
Keesler AFB, MS	2,519	U.S. Air Force Academy, CO	2,796
Kirtland AFB, NM	7,566	Vance AFB, OK	1,335
JB Langley-Eustis, VA	1,680	Vandenberg AFB, CA	1,577
Laughlin AFB, TX	4,487	Whiteman AFB, MO	2,641
JB Lewis-McChord, WA	3,214	Wright-Patterson AFB, OH	2,308

Assessing the Social and Economic Characteristics of Military Base Areas

This section describes how we applied social indicators methodology to the base areas, using survey data that capture objective characteristics about military and nonmilitary residents.

American Community Survey Data

The base areas we defined needed to be compatible with existing data on neighborhood and area characteristics. The types of indicators available at the city or county level are limited and are less likely to be comparable across cities or counties around the country. Neighborhood and area data, or social indicators data, at the ZIP Code, census-tract, or state level are far more prevalent.

We used the U.S. Census Bureau's American Community Survey (ACS) to gather social and economic indicators of area characteristics. This survey contains data sampled from all residents in the area, both military and nonmilitary, to capture community metrics. Because the ACS is a sample and not a census like the decennial census, each annual file is actually made up of a very small percentage of residents, especially at smaller geographic units. Thus, we used a five-year file, from 2005 to 2009, which aggregates data over time. Although the five-year aggregate file is not available at the ZIP Code level, it is available at the census-tract level. Census tracts contain roughly 4,000 residents, and a single county usually contains several tracts. ZIP Codes and census tracts do not overlap perfectly, but we used one of several existing databases that provide a crosswalk between the two.[10] Tracts were also weighted by overall population (not just Airmen) in order to make sure that those tracts that are more densely populated (and thus can have a greater impact on the populations and resources in their and neighboring communities) are weighted more heavily than those that are less densely populated.[11]

---

[10] More specifically, in order to match census tracts and ZIP Codes, a spatial weight matrix was created between the two geographies. Then, the social and economic characteristics of a census tract were apportioned to ZIP Codes in base areas in proportion to the percentage of the land area of the tracts that fell into a given ZIP code. That is, if 33 percent (or one-third) of a tract fell within the boundary of a ZIP, it was included in the definition of a base area.

[11] The results of the RAND BASE-I could vary if weighted instead by where Airmen are concentrated, especially if they are not evenly distributed across disadvantaged and privileged neighborhoods. However, weighting by overall population density makes sense because a densely populated tract could still influence Airmen or their families even if Airmen do not live precisely in that tract. Because people are not confined to the census tract or ZIP Codes in which they live, high rates of crime, unemployment, or poverty in one census tract could affect the safety, job prospects, and well-being resources available to people in adjacent or nearby areas. It is not necessary to reside in a specific neighborhood for it to have an effect on individual

From the ACS data file, we selected 20 indicators of social and economic area characteristics, grouped into six domains (see Table 2.3). These 20 indicators were selected for several reasons. First, as we noted in Chapter One, nearly all have been linked to individual health and well-being in the literature. An exception is the percentage of residents who are military veterans, which we include as an indicator of social cohesion given this study's focus on the relevance of these characteristics for a military population. Second, these items have been used in previous social indicators studies. And third, all can be quantified on a continuum from best to worst or least preferable to most preferable. We did not include any indicators that could not be ranked in this way (e.g., racial composition of an area). In Table 2.3, shaded cells indicate that a lower score is more favorable (e.g., unemployment rate, travel time).

---

outcomes. Nonetheless, the characteristics of the tracts where the *majority* of Airmen do live may be different from those where fewer reside. Thus, future work should revisit the decision of how to weight tracts and assess how the association between the RAND BASE-I and Airman outcomes differs when the tracts are weighted by Airman population instead of total population.

Table 2.3

The 20 Sociodemographic Census Indicators in the RAND Base Area Social and Economic Index, by Domain

Domain	Indicator
Household composition	Percentage of households headed by women
	Average household size
Housing	Percentage paying 35% or more of income for rent
	Percentage paying 35% or more of income for owner costs
	Percentage of housing units that are vacant
	Percentage of housing units that are renter occupied
	Percentage of residents living in the same house since the previous year
Employment	Percentage in labor force
	Percentage unemployed
Social	Percentage of residents with less than a high school diploma
	Percentage of residents with a bachelor's degree or higher
	Percentage of residents who are currently married
	Percentage of residents who are military veterans
Income and poverty	Median household income
	Mean public assistance amount
	Median family income[a]
	Percentage of families in poverty[a]
	Percentage of female-headed families in poverty[a]
Transportation	Mean travel time to work
	Percentage of residents with access to at least one automobile

NOTE: Shading indicates that lower scores are more favorable.
[a] Families are households in which at least one member is under the age of 18.

Household Composition

The household composition domain contains two indicators: the percentage of households headed by women and the average household size. Family members, especially children, fare better when family resources are distributed among fewer people (Bradbury, 1989; Downey, 1995). So, for our scoring process, the highest-scoring base areas will be those with the smallest average household size.[12] Similarly, female-headed households are typically characterized as lower in SES (i.e., income) (DeNavas-Walt, Proctor, and Smith, 2011), and children from these households fare worse on several well-being outcomes (McLanahan and Sandefur, 1996). Female-headed households have also been used as one dimension of neighborhood social disadvantage, and areas with a higher percentage of female-headed households have been linked to weakened community networks and lower levels of informal social control (see Sampson and Lauritsen, 1994).

Housing

The housing domain contains five indicators: percentage paying 35 percent or more of income for rent, percentage paying 35 percent or more of income for owner costs, percentage of housing units that are vacant, percentage of housing units that are occupied by renters, and percentage of people living in the same house since the previous year. The two indicators of spending on housing are indicators of the availability of affordable housing (or lack thereof), so higher scores are less favorable. Vacant housing units can be viewed as an indicator of several neighborhood characteristics, including residential turnover, economic well-being, and level of social cohesion (Coleman, 1990). Similarly, units occupied by renters and residential turnover, as measured by the percentage of residents living in the same house since the previous year, can also be seen as indicators of social cohesion. Higher percentages of housing units that are vacant or renter occupied are less favorable, whereas lower residential turnover is more favorable.

Employment

The employment domain contains two indicators: percentage in the labor force and percentage of people ages 16 and over who are unemployed. Employment rates can be considered a measure of neighborhood affluence, whereas unemployment rates represent neighborhood disadvantage. Note that labor force participation is not the opposite of unemployment. Unemployment calculations use only those who are looking for work. Neither of these measures accounts for underemployment or those who are working less than the desired number of hours or in jobs for which they are overqualified (McKee-Ryan and Harvey, 2011). Nor do they include individuals who are retired.

---

[12] Unfortunately, the census data we used cannot tell us whether the individuals in a household are adults or children.

Social

The social domain includes four indicators: percentage of individuals with less than a high school diploma, percentage with a bachelor's degree or higher, percentage currently married, and percentage who are military veterans. The two education indicators represent neighborhood disadvantage (i.e., less than a high school diploma) and affluence (i.e., college degree). As we noted above, children from two-parent families fare better on several outcomes than do their peers from single-parent families. Married households also tend to have higher SES (i.e., income) (DeNavas-Walt, Proctor, and Smith, 2011). We include the percentage of veterans as an indication of social cohesion among members of the military community, as well as community support for veterans (see Gates, 2010; Mullen, 2011). It may serve as a possible signal of community resources available to service members and their families. Higher percentages of college-educated residents, married families, and veterans are more favorable, whereas a higher percentage of high school–educated residents is less favorable.

Income and Poverty

The income and poverty domain has five indicators: mean household income, mean amount of public assistance received, median family income, percentage of families in poverty, and percentage of female-headed families in poverty. All of these indicators are standard measures of economic deprivation and general neighborhood disadvantage. The last three indicators focus specifically on the economic standing of families, defined as households with at least one child under the age of 18. Higher percentages on all five of these indicators are considered less favorable.

Transportation

The transportation domain includes two indicators: mean travel time to work and the percentage of residents with access to at least one automobile. Mean travel time, although an objective measure of neighborhood quality, is, in some ways, more like a subjective, QOL measure. Longer travel times are less favorable, with one study even linking longer work commute times to less access to social capital (Besser, Marcus, and Frumkin, 2008).[13] It is worth noting, however, that a longer commute time could also signal that an individual has the resources to live in a suburb of metropolitan area or on a ranch or farm

---

[13] Social capital in this 2008 study was operationalized as participating in socially oriented activities (e.g., sporting events, religious events, social events). Similarly, Putnam (2000) reports that every ten additional minutes of commute time results in a 10-percent decline in social capital.

in a more rural area.[14] If that is the case, then longer commute times could be viewed as more favorable to the individual. We took the more conventional view that more time spent in one's car leaves less time for family interaction and other activities and potentially increases risk for traffic accidents due to additional time on the road. Access to at least one automobile is viewed as a measure of SES, as well as wider employment and housing opportunities and ability to access community resources. As such, higher percentages of residents with access are viewed as more favorable.

We also note that the ACS data for each census tract in a base area are weighted by the population of that tract. Although census tracts are designed to have roughly the same population size in each, there is some variation. This weighting technique allows us to smooth that variation and ensure that more–densely populated tracts are not more influential in determining area characteristics than less densely populated tracts.

Data and Methods for Creating the Social and Economic Index Scores

The first part of this analysis used social indicators methodology to combine the base-area data into meaningful categories, or domains, in order to create installation profiles. For every characteristic, or indicator, shown in Table 2.3, we ordered base areas by comparing each area with the best-performing area on that specific indicator. For example, if the area surrounding base A has a 10-percent family poverty rate, the lowest, most desirable rate among all locations, but base B has a 15-percent poverty rate, then base A will receive a score of 100 (the highest score possible for an indicator) on the family poverty indicator, and base B will receive a score of 50 on the family poverty indicator. That is, base B's family poverty rate is 50 percent as good as the "best" (in this case, defined as the lowest) family poverty rate among all base areas. The "best" base area is always an actual area, not an ideal standard of zero poverty, zero unemployment, and so on. Indicator scores range from 100, which is set by the area with the most-desirable social conditions, and can reach into the negative range if a comparison area's performance is more than twice as poor as the best area.

The general indicator formula is presented below:

$$\text{RAND BASE-I} = \left(1 - \left[\frac{\text{best base-area score} - \text{current base-area score}}{\text{best base-area score}}\right]\right) \times 100.$$

---

[14] We did not include a measure of urbanicity in the index because the distinction between rural versus urban area is not clearly positive in one direction versus the other. That is, there is no clear way to objectively determine whether living in an urban area is "better" than living in a rural one (or vice versa).

The best score is the base area with the most desirable (highest or lowest) score on the indicator in question, and the current score is the base area that is being compared. The absolute value of the indicator score is then subtracted from 1. This value is then multiplied by 100. Thus, the result is one value for each indicator for each base area.

Once relative scores were calculated for the 20 social and economic indicators for each base area, they were then used to calculate a score for each area along each of the six domains of area indicators shown in Table 2.3: household composition, employment, transportation, social, income and poverty, and housing. The same methodology outlined above is used. For example, base A's scores on (1) gross rent as percentage of income, (2) owner costs as a percentage of income, (3) percentage of housing units that are vacant, and (4) percentage of housing units that are renter occupied are averaged into a single domain score for the housing domain. All of the indicators within a domain are weighted equally.[15] This process allows us to condense multiple base-area characteristics into one meaningful score for each domain of indicators.

Like indicator scores, domain scores can range from 100 to an unconstrained negative number. A score of 100 on a domain would reflect that a base area had the best score on all of the indicators within that domain. At no point in our analysis did a single area score best on every item within a domain, so a 100 domain score is a hypothetical score rather than an actual achieved score. It is important to note that the probability of achieving a "perfect" score within a domain is dependent on the number of items in the domain: The odds of a higher score are generally higher in a domain with fewer indicators (e.g., the employment domain versus the housing domain). Domain scores can generally be interpreted as how well a given base area is doing compared with a hypothetical area that scored the highest on all the indicators within a domain. Positive values can be interpreted as a percentage of the hypothetical area that receives an indicator score of 100; negative scores indicate that a base is doing more than twice as poorly.[16]

Finally, we created the RAND BASE-I. Scores across the six domains were averaged into a single, equally weighted index score. That is, each of the six domains listed in Table 2.3 carried equal weight in determining a base area's scoring. In turn, those six domains contain all of the 20 census-derived sociodemographic indicators, as shown in

---

[15] An alternative approach weights each of the 20 indicators equally, without calculating any domain scores. We refer to this scoring strategy as the RAND BASE-I(I), with the (I) denoting the direct use of the indicators. Results from this version of the RAND BASE-I appear in Appendix B. Results using both versions of the RAND BASE-I are substantively similar. Evidence from prior research suggests that, in the absence of a clear rationale for a preferred weighting scheme, an equally weighted *domain* index, rather than an equally weighted *indicator* index, is preferable (Hagerty and Land, 2007).

[16] Technically, a negative score can occur only for an indicator for which a lower number is better.

Figure 2.6. Thus, the RAND BASE-I indexes, or scores, each area against all other areas and allows us to condense base-area characteristics into a single meaningful set of scores.

Figure 2.6
Flow Chart for Derivation of RAND Base Area Social and Economic Index Score for Each Base Area

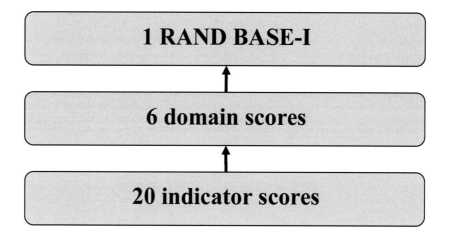

We refer to a score of 100 on the RAND BASE-I as a hypothetical gold standard for which areas might strive but never achieve. Similar to the interpretation of a domain score, the RAND BASE-I score tells us how well a particular base area is doing compared with a hypothetical area that scores the highest on all six domains and, thus, all 22 indicators. Because all scores are based on 100, the final RAND BASE-I score can be interpreted as a percentage of the hypothetical area (i.e., a score of 50 would mean that an area is doing 50 percent as well as the hypothetical base). For comparison purposes, Table 2.4 reviews the similarities and differences among the three different measures that can be used to score base areas.

The results of the RAND BASE-I are reported and discussed in Chapter Three. The next section of this chapter describes the data and methods behind Chapters Four and Five.

Table 2.4
Description of Measures by Which Base Areas Can Be Assessed

Score	Description	Data Points	Highest Possible Score	Lowest Possible Score	Interpretation of Score
Indicator	Population-weighted average of a single census social or economic characteristic, indexed against other base areas	20	100	Unconstrained negative value identifying how far below the best actual indicator score a base area falls	Percentage of best base-area indicator score
Domain	Equally weighted average of multiple indicator scores that fall within a particular substantive domain	6	100	Unconstrained negative value identifying how far below the highest possible domain score a base area falls	Percentage of hypothetical base area that scores highest on all indicators within a domain
RAND BASE-I	Equally weighted average of all domain scores	1	100	Unconstrained negative value identifying how far below the highest possible RAND BASE-I score a base area falls	Percentage of hypothetical base area that scores highest on all domains

Before moving on to a description of how we used the RAND BASE-I, it is important to point out a potential limitation of its construction. Although each domain is equally weighted in the sense that all are summed and divided by their total (i.e., six), the *variances* of each of the indicators that make up each domain are not weighted equally. For example, the range between the highest and lowest scores on the percentage of each base area that has access to an automobile is much smaller than the range of scores for mean public assistance dollars. Thus, some of the rescaled RAND BASE-I indicators have higher variance than other indicators, and the overall RAND BASE-I is dominated by those indicators with larger variances. In some ways, this does make this construction of the RAND BASE-I more difficult to interpret because variances of the 20 indicators are not standardized before they are used in the index. The difficulty in interpretation manifests itself primarily among the indicators for which lower scores are better and for which index scores can fall below zero. In Appendix B, we calculate an alternative version of the RAND BASE-I, called the RAND BASE-I(Z), for which we use a z-score transformation to constrain variances of the indicators. We offer this alternative specification to show that there is no one "right" way to construct an index of this sort. We opted to use a technique that is standard in the social indicators literature, but other transformation and index procedures are available, and future work should examine how those alternative indices may be associated with Airman outcomes.

Multilevel Modeling to Assess Links Between the RAND Base Area Social and Economic Index and Airman Outcomes on Two Surveys

After defining the base area and creating the social indicators index, we used a specialized regression technique to analyze whether this index was associated with self-reported Airman outcomes on two surveys conducted by the Air Force.

Survey Data

We used data from two Air Force–sponsored surveys to assess the association between base-area characteristics (i.e., the RAND BASE-I) and Airmen's responses to items on health and well-being, military and neighborhood social cohesion, neighborhood resources, use of on-base resources, satisfaction, and career intentions. First, we used the 2011 Air Force Community Assessment Survey. The survey was designed to help senior Air Force leadership determine the strengths and needs of Air Force communities and to help service providers effectively utilize installation-specific resources. It has been conducted, Air Force–wide, every two to three years since 1988–1989. The Community Assessment Survey uses a stratified random sampling technique to capture a representative sample of Airmen, spouses, and civilians by base. The firm ICF International administered the anonymous survey from January through March 2011 via the web. Although the Community Assessment Survey contains survey data from both active-duty and reserve Airmen, their spouses, and civilians, we limited our analysis to only active-duty and reserve Airmen to ensure that sample sizes per subpopulation per base were large enough to support the analysis.[17] Approximately 64,000 active-duty Airmen and 7,000 reserve Airmen completed the survey, for a response rate of 40 percent and 42 percent, respectively. Because the survey was fielded at 105 different bases, some of which were outside the continental United States (OCONUS), our actual analysis

---

[17] Given the potential for increased interaction with and exposure to the neighborhood or area, neighborhood and area factors may have an even larger association with spouse and family outcomes than with Airmen's own outcomes. As noted, the sample size of spouses per base in the Community Assessment Survey was too small to support our analysis, but we recommend that this be a topic for future research.

sample for our selected installations is smaller.[18] Using the base assignment variable from the survey, we matched Airmen to the appropriate base area in the RAND BASE-I.

The second data set we used was the 2010 Caring for People Survey. The survey was designed to assess how Air Force leaders could better address the health and well-being needs of active-duty, reserve, and guard Airmen, civilians, retirees, and spouses. Data were collected from December 2010 through January 2011 via the web. Again, we restricted our analysis to active-duty and reserve Airmen. Unlike the Community Assessment Survey, the Caring for People Survey did not sample by base. However, participants were asked to provide both their base assignments and their ZIP Codes. We relied on self-reported ZIP Codes to then match Airmen to the base areas in our index, supplementing with base assignment only if a ZIP was not available.

The use of Air Force–sponsored surveys has benefits. First, both surveys allowed us to connect Airmen to an installation and thus to a base area. Second, the data contain outcomes about Airmen, particularly the proximate and distal outcomes shown in Figure 1.1 in Chapter One, that are important to the Air Force. In this way, our use of the data fits well with the intentions of the survey. Third, both surveys are well-known by Airmen. Fourth, the use of existing data-collection efforts, versus creating and fielding our own survey, reduced the survey burden on Airmen. Fifth, although similar in some ways, the two surveys covered complementary but largely different areas. For example, the Community Assessment Survey covered more topics related to health and well-being, whereas the Caring for People Survey covered service utilization.

Conversely, the Community Assessment Survey and Caring for People Survey data also have drawbacks. First, as with any secondary data analysis, some of the items we used were not ideal for our purposes. Slight wording changes, different response category options, or different skip patterns could make a difference in the results. Second, although sample sizes are large enough to support our analysis, response rates were not high. This introduces the possibility of bias in the data if certain types of Airmen (e.g., younger, single parents, less satisfied) did not complete the survey. Third, as with most survey data, it is possible that negative outcomes, especially those associated with mental or behavioral health, may be underreported, even though this is an anonymous survey. If this is the case, the association between neighborhood characteristics and the more-distal outcomes in which the Air Force is interested may be downwardly biased. Despite these potential limitations, the Community Assessment Survey and the Caring for People Survey data offer the best opportunity to link important Airman outcomes to neighborhood quality.

---

[18] We provide analysis sample sizes in Chapter Three.

A Multilevel Modeling Approach

The second part of the analysis assessed the association between the RAND BASE-I and individual Airman well-being outcomes. To do so, we used a multilevel model: individuals at one level and the base areas at the second level. This type of modeling strategy was used for two reasons. First, it allowed us to estimate the correct standard error of the association between neighborhood characteristics and outcomes. The standard error can be thought of as the amount of error around our estimates. If the multilevel nature of the data is not taken into account, the size of this error will be underestimated, thereby making it more likely that we will find results that are statistically significant (i.e., false positives). Second, the covariates we introduced into the models may also vary across bases. If they do, then the associations we observed between any given domain or the overall RAND BASE-I and the outcomes may simply be due to installation differences in the covariates.

We note that some of the base areas substantially overlapped, as, for example, was the case with bases that are located in the National Capital region (e.g., JB Anacostia-Bolling, JB Andrews-NAF Washington, the Pentagon). The implication of this overlap is that, in our multilevel models, the actual number of independent observations may not exactly equal the number of bases. If this is the case, then our significance tests might slightly overstate statistical significance. As a result, we focused not only on statistical significance but also on practical significance through the use of effect sizes.

When possible, we ran models separately for active-duty and reserve Airmen. Airmen in the reserve and guard generally do not live on base. Among active-duty Airmen, we also tested for an interaction between living on base and the RAND BASE-I and its six constituent domains, each entered independently (i.e., one domain at a time). If the association between the RAND BASE-I or domains and the outcome in question were significantly different for those Airmen who live on base and their off-base peers, then this interaction should be statistically significant. If this were the case, we further tested separate models for on- and off-base Airmen. The results of the multilevel modeling for the Community Assessment Survey are presented in Chapter Four, and the results for the Caring for People Survey are presented in Chapter Five.

Conclusion

This chapter described the data and methods for each of the analyses presented in the next three chapters. We developed a base-area definition that applied approaches from the neighborhood studies literature to the area including and surrounding 66 military installations in the United States with a sizable Air Force population. We also applied an established social indicators methodology to develop an index for these base areas, using a data set collected by the U.S. Census Bureau and commonly used for social indicators research. Finally, we used a specialized regression technique known as multilevel modeling to explore whether there were links between the social indicators index and outcomes on two Air Force surveys.

Chapter Three. The RAND Base Area Social and Economic Index

The first step in our analysis plan was to compute a social indicators RAND BASE-I score for each of the 66 AFBs included in the study. Recall that RAND BASE-I scores are *relative*, not absolute. That is, we are always comparing one base area with another, typically whichever neighborhood performs the highest (or lowest) on a specific indicator. We must also emphasize that we calculated a ranking of social and economic indicators for the military and nonmilitary populations living in these base areas, which includes both the base and the surrounding area. Thus, this index reports characteristics for regions and populations outside of Air Force control. The RAND BASE-I is not a ranking of the quality of on-base facilities and resources, nor does it convey the QOL of Airmen and their families, who fare better than some of their fellow residents who may be unemployed, lack health insurance, or even lack housing. Also, this index is not a list of most and least desirable places to live. Airman preferences for base assignments may take into account many factors not captured in this analysis (e.g., climate, population density, urbanicity, proximity to extended family and friends, career opportunities for Airmen or for spouses, and quality of base facilities and resources).

The objective of this ranking index is to help the Air Force identify where there might be a greater need for Air Force support for Airmen and their families due to more-stressful living conditions or a lack of nonmilitary community resources. The index can also help identify relatively resource-rich areas where Air Force Services may be redundant with resources in the surrounding community and thus could potentially be scaled back or redirected.

Overall RAND Base Area Social and Economic Index Results

Table 3.1 presents the scores of all 66 base areas, using the RAND BASE-I with equally weighted domains.[19] The highest-scoring base area is the one that includes the Pentagon, located in Virginia near Washington, D.C., with an index score of 62.7. Other base areas that scored high include the area including and surrounding Minot AFB, North

---

[19] In Appendix B, we also present the RAND BASE-I for base areas defined as 30- and 90-minute boundaries, as well as the RAND BASE-I with equally weighted *indicators* using the 60-minute boundary. Recall that this indicator version of the RAND BASE-I in the appendix equally weights each of the 20 indicators versus equally weighting the six domains.

Dakota (62.3); JB Anacostia-Bolling, Washington, D.C. (59.6); Fort George Meade, Maryland (58.1); and the U.S. Air Force Academy, Colorado (57.8). Note that none of the base areas scored a perfect 100 on the RAND BASE-I. This indicates that, although these areas scored well (relative to other areas), none was ranked highest (or lowest) on all 20 indicators. Recall that this index measures factors that are outside of the control of the Air Force, such as unemployment rates, vacant-housing rates, average household size, and education level of the general populace. The index is not a system that "grades" installations but a way of capturing area characteristics that may have an impact on service members and their families.

Also note that three of the highest-scoring base areas—JB Anacostia-Bolling, the Pentagon, and Fort George Meade—contain installations not controlled by the Air Force. These installations are included in our analysis because of the large presence of Airmen at these locations. Even though the Air Force may have limited ability to make changes at these bases, the experience of Airmen assigned there and the policies and practices used at those installations may provide useful examples for the Air Force to consider.

Table 3.1
RAND Base Area Social and Economic Index for 66 Air Force Base Areas

Base Area	RAND BASE-I	Base Area	RAND BASE-I
Altus AFB, OK	10.1	Little Rock AFB, AR	16.4
JB Anacostia-Bolling, DC	59.6	Los Angeles AFB, CA	33.5
JB Andrews-NAF Washington, MD	55.9	Luke AFB, AZ	15.0
Arnold AFB, TN	−8.1	MacDill AFB, FL	7.3
Barksdale AFB, LA	4.6	Malmstrom AFB, MT	18.6
Beale AFB, CA	−2.8	Maxwell AFB, AL	−20.9
Buckley AFB, CO	47.0	McConnell AFB, KS	44.3
Cannon AFB, NM	24.7	JB McGuire-Dix-Lakehurst, NJ	35.0
JB Charleston, SC	−12.9	Minot AFB, ND	62.3
Columbus AFB, MS	−33.8	Moody AFB, GA	3.5
Creech AFB, NV	20.2	Mountain Home AFB, ID	−2.0
Davis-Monthan AFB, AZ	32.5	Nellis AFB, NV	23.0
Dover AFB, DE	1.2	Offutt AFB, NE	52.3
Dyess AFB, TX	22.1	Patrick AFB, FL	17.7
Edwards AFB, CA	−64.6	JB Pearl Harbor–Hickam, HI	25.0
Eglin AFB, FL	9.8	Pentagon, VA	62.7
Eielson AFB, AK	17.4	Peterson AFB, CO	50.3
Ellsworth AFB, SD	36.8	Pope Field, NC	−17.1
JB Elmendorf-Richardson, AK	4.7	Robins AFB, GA	−2.8
Fairchild AFB, WA	20.8	JB San Antonio, TX	16.4
F. E. Warren AFB, WY	40.1	Schriever AFB, CO	52.5
Fort George G. Meade, MD	58.1	Scott AFB, IL	15.7
Goodfellow AFB, TX	19.8	Seymour Johnson AFB, NC	−12.9
Grand Forks AFB, ND	56.4	Shaw AFB, SC	−22.2
Hanscom AFB, MA	41.2	Sheppard AFB, TX	5.3
Hill AFB, UT	48.2	Tinker AFB, OK	17.2
Holloman AFB, NM	−28.7	Travis AFB, CA	8.0
Hurlburt Field, FL	0.1	Tyndall AFB, FL	−11.3
Keesler AFB, MS	−7.3	U.S. Air Force Academy, CO	57.8
Kirtland AFB, NM	14.9	Vance AFB, OK	5.3
JB Langley-Eustis, VA	24.4	Vandenberg AFB, CA	9.6
Laughlin AFB, TX	−38.2	Whiteman AFB, MO	20.8
JB Lewis-McChord, WA	11.7	Wright-Patterson AFB, OH	18.0

NOTE: The RAND BASE-I contains 20 indicators of the social and economic characteristics of the area within a 60-mile radius around a base. The Air Force cannot control these characteristics (e.g., unemployment rates, vacant-housing rates, education level of the general populace), but it can consider their potential impact on Airmen and their families. The RAND BASE-I should not be viewed as an indicator of absolute neighborhood quality or as an indicator of "most-preferred places to live."

37

Turning to the areas with the lowest scores, we see that the area that includes Edwards AFB in California scores lowest with an overall index score, or RAND BASE-I score, of –64.6. An overall negative score on the RAND BASE-I indicates that the area in question is struggling on multiple indicators, not just one. Other low-scoring areas also have indicators scores well below zero, including the areas that contain Laughlin AFB, Texas (–38.2), Columbus AFB, Mississippi (–33.8), Holloman AFB, New Mexico (–28.7), and Shaw AFB, South Carolina (–22.2).

RAND Base Area Social and Economic Index Domain Results

We shift now to the six constituent domains in the RAND BASE-I: household composition, employment, income and poverty, housing, social, and transportation. Table 3.2 shows the correlations between the six domains. In general, the correlation matrix suggests that economic indicators are driving the overall RAND BASE-I. The correlations between the employment domain (rho = 0.82) and the income and poverty domain (rho = 0.93) and the overall RAND BASE-I are both very high and statistically significant. However, the household composition domain (rho = 0.78) and the social domain (rho = 0.73) are also highly correlated with the overall RAND BASE-I, suggesting that the index is picking up characteristics of areas that are not only economic. The housing domain (rho = 0.50) is less strongly correlated with the RAND BASE-I but still makes a contribution.

The transportation domain (rho = 0.02) is very weakly correlated with the RAND BASE-I, and this correlation is not statistically significant. As we note below, the variance in this domain is quite small because the vast majority of area residents across all areas indicate that they have access to an automobile. Note also the moderate, statistically significant correlation between the transportation domain and the employment domain (rho = 0.30). The correlation is not surprising given that one of the indicators in the transportation domain is commute time to work. Employment status may also be a prerequisite for being able to afford and maintain a working automobile. Thus, the contribution of the transportation domain may be working through the employment domain.

Table 3.2
Correlations Between the Six Constituent Domains and the RAND Base Area Social and Economic Index

Domain	1	2	3	4	5	6	7
1. RAND BASE-I		0.78	0.82	0.93	0.50	0.73	0.02[a]
2. Household composition			0.69	0.50	0.36	0.62	0.09[a]
3. Employment				0.61	0.27	0.46	0.30
4. Income and poverty					0.32	0.59	−0.15[a]
5. Housing						0.15[a]	−0.13[a]
6. Social							−0.22[a]
7. Transportation							

[a] Correlation is not statistically significant at the p < 0.05 level.

We also see evidence that the social and economic domains are related. For example, the household composition domain is strongly correlated with both the income and poverty domain (rho = 0.50) and the employment domain (rho = 0.69). The social domain is also strongly correlated with the income and poverty domain (rho = 0.59) and moderately correlated with the employment domain (rho = 0.46). This gives us more confidence that the RAND BASE-I is actually measuring both the economic and social climates of base areas.

Household Composition Domain

The household composition domain contains two indicators: percentage of households that are headed by women and the average household size. Table 3.3 shows the top and bottom five base areas on this domain.[20] Not surprisingly, the five top- and bottom-scoring base areas on the domain look very similar to the top and bottom five areas on the overall RAND BASE-I. One thing to note in this domain is that the top-scoring areas score quite high. This indicates that bases that score high on one indicator in the domain also score high on the other (i.e., low percentage of households headed by women and lower household sizes). The areas at the bottom end of the distribution have negative scores, meaning that their values on both of the indicators in the domain scores are well below those of the top-ranked areas.

---

[20] Full scores for each of the six domains can be found in Appendix C.

Table 3.3
Domain-Specific Results: Household Composition Domain

Top Five Areas		Bottom Five Areas	
Area	Score	Area	Score
1. Grand Forks AFB, ND	94.86	62. Pope Field, NC	−9.25
2. Minot AFB, ND	89.76	63. JB Charleston, SC	−21.93
3. Cannon AFB, NM	72.77	64. Maxwell AFB, AL	−23.52
4. Hill AFB, UT	72.44	65. Columbus AFB, MS	−25.54
5. U.S. Air Force Academy, CO	71.91	66. Shaw AFB, SC	−31.75

NOTE: The household composition domain contains two indicators: percentage of households headed by women and average household size.

Employment Domain

The employment domain is made up of two indicators: the percentage of area residents in the labor force and the percentage of area residents who are unemployed. The results for the domain are shown in Table 3.4. Again, we see some consistency across the top and bottom five base areas. We also see that the top base areas have high, positive scores, indicating that these areas do well on both indicators in the domain. The bottom areas, however, have low scores, showing that these areas do poorly on both indicators.

Table 3.4
Domain-Specific Results: Employment Domain

Top Five Areas		Bottom Five Areas	
Area	Score	Area	Score
1. Minot AFB, ND	96.73	62. Beale AFB, CA	−48.28
2. Vance AFB, OK	80.45	63. Arnold AFB, TN	−53.17
3. Grand Forks AFB, ND	78.23	64. Shaw AFB, SC	−54.89
4. Cannon AFB, NM	71.91	65. Columbus AFB, MS	−66.26
5. Pentagon, VA	64.82	66. Edwards AFB, CA	−81.99

NOTE: The employment domain contains two indicators: percentage in labor force and percentage unemployed.

Income and Poverty Domain

Table 3.5 shows the top and bottom five base areas in the income and poverty domain. This domain is made up of five indicators: median household income, mean amount of public assistance, median family income, the percentage of families in the area who are in poverty, and the percentage of female-headed households in the area that are in poverty. The most notable finding here is the large spread of the domain scores. The highest-scoring base area, that around the Pentagon, scored roughly 77. The lowest-scoring base area, that around Edwards AFB in California, scored –358.62. To score as poorly as the bottom five areas do, they must score poorly on most of the indicators in the domain. Three indicators appear to be especially problematic: reliance on large amounts of public assistance, the family poverty rate, and the poverty rate of female-headed families. Remember, the rates come from a sample of the entire population in these areas, not just military families.

Table 3.5
Domain-Specific Results: Income and Poverty Domain

Top Five Areas		Bottom Five Areas	
Area	Score	Area	Score
1. Pentagon, VA	76.98	62. Mountain Home AFB, ID	–160.69
2. JB Anacostia-Bolling, DC	76.55	63. Columbus AFB, MS	–176.69
3. JB Andrews-NAF Washington MD	67.34	64. Vance AFB, OK	–194.27
4. Fort George Meade, MD	56.99	65. Holloman AFB, NM	–196.16
5. U.S. Air Force Academy, CO	21.60	66. Edwards AFB, CA	–358.62

NOTE: The income and poverty domain contains five indicators: median household income, mean amount of public assistance, median family income, percentage of families in poverty, and percentage of female-headed households in poverty.

To put the impact of these indicators into more-meaningful terms, we provide three examples. First, residents in the Patrick AFB area in Florida use an average of $14 in public assistance per month. In contrast, residents in the Edwards AFB area in California use roughly $220 in public assistance.[21] This means that the range of index scores on this single indicator is from 100, for the Patrick AFB area, to –1,404, for the area around Edwards AFB. Second, family poverty rates vary from a low of 2.5 percent in the Pentagon base area to a high of 24 percent for the Holloman AFB area in New Mexico. Thus, the range in index scores for the family poverty rate indicator is 100 to –746. And third, the family poverty rate among female-headed households in the JB Anacostia-Bolling area in Washington, D.C., is 11 percent. In contrast, in the Vance AFB area in

---

[21] It is important to keep in mind that this does *not* mean that Airmen and their families utilize this amount of public assistance, or any assistance for that matter. Census-tract information is a weighted average of values for all residents within the tract.

Oklahoma, that percentage is just over 60. Index scores on this indicator range from 100 to –335.

Housing Domain

The housing domain includes five indicators: the percentage of area residents spending 35 percent or more of their income on rent or housing costs (these are two separate indicators), the percentage of housing units that are vacant, the percentage of housing units occupied by renters, and the percentage living in the same house since the previous year. Table 3.6 presents the top and bottom five base areas on the housing domain. Compared with scores on the income and poverty domain, the spread between top and bottom scores on this domain is much narrower. However, we do see evidence that base areas that score high on one indicator with the domain also score well on the others (i.e., top scores are positive and relatively high). Yet, because the top end of the domain does not have scores at 100, or scores that are as high as those in the household composition and employment domains, there is greater variance at the top than occurs in some of the other domains. Lower domain scores are driven primarily by the percentage of housing units that are vacant and by spending on housing.

Table 3.6
Domain-Specific Results: Housing Domain

Top Five Areas		Bottom Five Areas	
Area	**Score**	**Area**	**Score**
1. McConnell AFB, KS	69.85	62. Laughlin AFB, TX	–43.18
2. Offutt AFB, NE	65.61	63. Edwards AFB, CA	–46.63
3. Fort George Meade, MD	63.42	64. Holloman AFB, NM	–48.45
4. Whiteman AFB, MO	60.53	65. Hurlburt Field, FL	–62.49
5. U.S. Air Force Academy, CO	58.22	66. Tyndall AFB, FL	–90.18

NOTE: The housing domain contains five indicators: percentage paying 35% or more of income in rent, percentage paying 35% or more of income in owner costs, percentage of housing units that are vacant, percentage of housing units that are renter occupied, and percentage of residents living in the same house since the previous year.

Social Domain

Table 3.7 presents the results for the social domain, which includes four indicators: the percentage of area residents with less than a high school degree, the percentage with a bachelor's degree or more, the percentage who are currently married, and the percentage who are veterans. It is perhaps not surprising that a base area that includes a university,

42

the Air Force Academy, scores highest on the domain that includes indicators of educational attainment. In contrast, residents living in the Laughlin AFB area in Texas are much less educated: Only 16 percent have a bachelor's degree or higher (compared with 44 percent in the academy's base area), whereas 33 percent have less than a high school degree (compared with an amazing 99 percent in the academy's base area).

Table 3.7
Domain-Specific Results: Social Domain

Top Five Areas		Bottom Five Areas	
Area	Score	Area	Score
1. U.S. Air Force Academy, CO	85.63	62. Seymour Johnson AFB, NC	−40.81
2. Eielson AFB, AK	81.29	63. Columbus AFB, CS	−41.42
3. Schriever AFB, CO	81.02	64. Goodfellow AFB, TX	−47.21
4. Peterson AFB, CO	78.58	65. Cannon AFB, NM	−50.68
5. Pentagon, VA	70.71	66. Laughlin AFB, TX	−115.29

NOTE: The social domain contains four indicators: percentage with less than a high school degree, percentage with a bachelor's degree or higher, percentage currently married, and percentage who are military veterans.

Transportation Domain

The final domain is the transportation domain, which contains two indicators: mean travel time to work and the percentage with access to at least one automobile. The Cannon AFB area in New Mexico has the highest score on the index at 99.26 (see Table 3.8). JB Anacostia-Bolling's base area in Washington, D.C., has the lowest domain score at 41.36. This represents a departure from the other domains, on which the lowest domain score has always been a negative score. The primary reason for this is that the variance on one of the indicators is very small: The difference between the highest and lowest percentage of residents who have access to an automobile is 3 percent (99.6 percent for the Ellsworth AFB area in South Dakota and 96.5 percent for the Moody AFB area in Georgia). Mean travel time to work has more variability but still varies over only roughly 15 minutes (15 minutes for the Cannon AFB area in New Mexico and 32 minutes for the JB Anacostia-Bolling AFB area in Washington, D.C.).

Table 3.8
Domain-Specific Results: Transportation Domain

Top Five Areas		Bottom Five Areas	
Area	**Score**	**Area**	**Score**
1. Cannon AFB, NM	99.26	62. JB McGuire-Dix-Lakehurst, NJ	53.20
2. Minot AFB, ND	97.49	63. Fort George Meade, MD	46.36
3. Eielson AFB, AK	95.77	64. JB Andrews-NAF Washington, MD	42.87
4. Altus AFB, OK	94.85	65. Pentagon, VA	42.83
5. Grand Forks AFB, ND	92.24	66. JB Anacostia-Bolling, DC	41.36

NOTE: The transportation domain contains two indicators: mean travel time to work and percentage with access to at least one automobile.

Interestingly, for the transportation domain, the highest-scoring areas on the overall RAND BASE-I score poorly on this domain. Many of the D.C.-area base areas—JB Andrews-NAF Washington, the Pentagon, and JB Anacostia-Bolling—have longer commute times, which results in lower scores on the index. But these same areas have much higher scores on other indicators, and domains, which results in higher overall scores on the overall RAND BASE-I.

Omitted Indicator Variables

As noted in Chapter Two, there are other census data that we could have included in the RAND BASE-I. For some indicators, such as the racial and ethnic composition of the area, we did not include them because it is not obvious which direction to order them (e.g., is having a smaller or larger minority presence "good" or "bad"?). Other examples include measures of population density, urbanicity, and region. It is possible that one or more of these omitted indicator variables may actually be driving the other indicators that we did use in the RAND BASE-I. Thus, we examined the degree to which omitted variables may account for variation in the RAND BASE-I. Those omitted indicators include the following:

- region (e.g., Northeast, South, Midwest, West)
- racial and ethnic composition: percentage minority, percentage Hispanic, percentage non-Hispanic black
- total population
- square mileage
- population density: total population per square mile

- urbanicity: urban cluster (UC), urban area (UA), rural[22]
- Air Force MAJCOM: Air Education and Training Command (AETC), Air Force Materiel Command (AFMC), Air Combatant Command (ACC), Air Force Global Strike Command (AFGSC), Air Force Space Command (AFSPC), Air Mobility Command (AMC), Air Force Special Operations Command (AFSOC), Pacific Air Forces (PACAF).[23]

Table 3.9 shows amount of variance in the RAND BASE-I that can be explained by the omitted variables. In general, the amount of variance explained is in the moderate range, with some characteristics accounting for a larger amount of variation than others. Looking at the columns for the adjusted R^2, two of the three race and ethnicity indicators (percentage minority and percentage Hispanic) can explain less than 10 percent of the variance in the RAND BASE-I. The same is true for total population, square mileage, population density, and all three measures of urbanicity (UC, UA, and rural).

---

[22] The Census Bureau defines a UA as an area with a population of 50,000 or more; a UC has a population between 2,500 and 49,999; a rural area is defined as any that is not included in an urban area. An urbanized area serves as the core of a metropolitan statistical area (MSA), while a UC serves as the core of a micropolitan statistical area (see U.S. Census Bureau, 2010).

[23] We matched installations to primary MAJCOM using the 2009 *USAF Almanac* (see U.S. Air Force, 2009). An installation can fall under more than one command.

Table 3.9
Correlations Between Omitted Indicators and the RAND Base Area Social and Economic Index

Indicator	RAND BASE-I R^2	Adjusted R^2
Region	0.16	0.10
Racial and ethnic composition		
Percentage minority	0.09	0.07
Percentage Hispanic	0.03	0.02
Percentage non-Hispanic black	0.13	0.11
Total population	0.12	0.10
Square mileage	0.03	0.01
Population density	0.07	0.05
Urbanicity		
UC	0.01	−0.01
UA	0.07	0.05
Rural	0.06	0.04
Air Force MAJCOM	0.36	0.10

NOTE: Adjusted for clustering at base level.

Three variables—percentage non-Hispanic black, region, and command—do have adjusted R^2 values at 0.10 or higher. As we noted above, we did not include race and ethnicity composition in the RAND BASE-I given that is not obvious whether minority presence is universally positive or negative in terms of individual-level outcomes. As we noted above, the results of the RAND BASE-I do seem to cluster geographically, with base areas in the South generally scoring lower on the index than base areas in other regions of the country. Although an R^2 of 0.10 indicates some correlation between the RAND BASE-I and region, we remind the reader that this still leaves much variance unexplained.

An installation's primary MAJCOM also explained roughly 10 percent of the variance in RAND BASE-I scores. This is not necessarily surprising given that certain types of installations need to be located in certain types of areas (e.g., bases where Airmen must get flight time must have space to house aircraft, build runways, and not disturb local residents). Thus, command and region may be tapping into the same underlying construct. When thinking about the results presented in the remainder of the report, it will be important to keep in mind that some of these omitted indicator variables may also be contributing to the associations we find between the RAND BASE-I and Airman outcomes.

Conclusions

Overall, we can draw four main conclusions from the results of the RAND BASE-I scoring exercise. First, there is quite a bit of variability in area characteristics on most of the dimensions measured for each of the base areas, meaning there is quite a gap between the characteristics of the areas at the top of the index and those on the bottom. Second, the top-scoring base areas do show some geographic clustering, particularly around the Washington, D.C., area (i.e., JB Anacostia-Bolling, the Pentagon, Fort George Meade, JB Andrews-NAF Washington), North Dakota (i.e., Minot and Grand Forks), and Colorado (i.e., U.S. Air Force Academy and Schriever). Similar clustering at the bottom end of the RAND BASE-I is not apparent; however, the South does not tend to do well. Only one base area in the southern United States is ranked in the top half of the RAND BASE-I. The base area that includes Patrick AFB, located in Florida, scores 31st on the overall index.

Third, economic and social resources appear to be clustered based on geography. For example, of the six domains that include some type of economic indicator (e.g., employment, income and poverty, housing), all have a wider distribution of indicator and domain index scores. This means that the lowest-scoring areas perform extremely poorly, having large, negative scores. In particular, poverty rates, especially those among families, and reliance on public-assistance dollars are drivers of these extreme negative domain scores. Further, some areas of the country have been more (or less) affected by the recent economic recession (see Martin, 2010).

Fourth, although neighborhood studies have primarily relied on economic indicators as a representation of neighborhood quality, noneconomic indicators of neighborhood well-being may also be important for QOL. In the RAND BASE-I, these indicators include higher education levels, lower commute times, more married families, and low residential turnover. As we showed in Table 3.2, some of these more-social indicators are often correlated with more–purely economic indicators and together can provide a more well-rounded and complete picture of community well-being and resources that may be available to community members.

In the next two chapters, we present results from multilevel models in which scores on the RAND BASE-I and its constituent domains are used to predict outcomes among Airmen and their families. These models account for clustering of Airmen within base areas. We begin with results from the 2011 Community Assessment Survey, followed by results from the 2010 Caring for People Survey.

47

Chapter Four. Linking the RAND Base Area Social and Economic Index to Airman Outcomes: The 2011 Community Assessment Survey

This chapter presents the results from a multilevel analysis of the 2011 Community Assessment Survey. The modeling technique allows us to assess the association between the RAND BASE-I and its constituent domains and Airman outcomes at the individual level while controlling for the fact that those Airmen are "nested" within specific bases.[24] We start by describing the sample, then describe the outcomes we considered in the analysis, and finally present a summary of the results of the multilevel modeling on whether any associations with the RAND BASE-I were found. We report only those associations that were statistically significant in the full model (i.e., the model that includes control variables): If the association is not described in this chapter, then it was not significant.

Sample Description

Although the Community Assessment Survey did not record ZIP Code information about where Airmen lived, it did record base assignment data, which we use to match Airmen to base areas. The survey also requested self-reported data on how far Airmen lived from their current base assignments.[25] Although the match between our 60-minute driving-radius definition of a base area and the distance categories in miles in the survey is not perfect, it does give some indication of how many survey respondents may live in the base areas as we have defined them. Among all active-duty Airmen in our analytic sample, roughly 70 percent lived within ten miles of their assigned bases, 20 percent lived between 10 and 20 miles away, and the remaining 10 percent lived more than 20 miles away. Among the reserve Airmen in our analytic sample, roughly two-thirds lived within 50 miles of their assigned bases, while the remaining one-third lived more than 50 miles away. Obviously, there is some variation around these averages (see Tables D.1

---

[24] The base area for Arnold AFB was dropped from the analysis because no Airmen in the survey data reported that they were assigned to those bases.

[25] Note that the Community Assessment Survey did not allow respondents to respond with any distance but rather required that they select the appropriate category. Category options differed for active duty and reserve.

and D.2 in Appendix D). For example, among the reserve, 100 percent of our sample lived within 50 miles of Dyess AFB near Abilene, Texas. However, at Minot AFB in North Dakota, 100 percent of our sample lived more than 50 miles away.

Active Duty

The majority of Airmen responding to the survey were male, enlisted (at the rank of E5 or E6), under the age of 35, married, with one or two children.[26] Just over 8 percent had a family member with some type of special need. In terms of living arrangements, roughly two-thirds lived off base, and, of those, almost two-thirds lived within ten miles of the base. Roughly equal percentages owned their own homes versus renting.

We also include two health and well-being variables in our description of the sample because they are included as control variables in our multilevel models. The first is a single survey item that asked, "How well do you cope with stress in your daily life?" Answers ranged from "extremely poorly" (1) to "extremely well" (7). We refer to this as self-rated coping. The average score on self-rated coping was just under 6 (roughly "well"), indicating that Airmen believed that they were able to handle daily stress and strain.

Second, we include a measure of self-rated resilience. The original Connor-Davidson Resilience Scale (CD-RISC) (Connor and Davidson, 2003) contained 25 items and was designed to help quantify resilience as a clinical measure to assess treatment response. It has been used primarily in adolescent samples but shows good psychometric properties. An abbreviated, ten-item version of the CD-RISC, called the CD-RISC 2, has been proposed by Campbell-Sills and Stein (2007), who have validated the measure using undergraduate samples. The proprietary CD-RISC 2 was used in the Community Assessment Survey. The ten items assess attitudes toward stress and adversity as well as survey participants' beliefs about how they respond to such challenges. Each item was rated on a scale from "not at all true" (1) to "true nearly all the time" (5). On average, Airmen rated themselves very highly on the CD-RISC 2, with a mean score of 4.2.

We also compared the demographic profiles of Airmen who lived on versus off base. On and off base, active-duty Airmen looked very similar on most characteristics, with one exception. Younger, lower-ranking enlisted Airmen were more likely to live on base. For example, of Airmen who lived off base, only 16 percent of enlisted Airmen were between the ranks of E1 and E4. Of Airmen who lived on base, 43 percent were E1 to E4.

---

[26] A detailed table of demographic statistics for active-duty Airmen in the analytic sample can be found in Table D.3 in Appendix D.

Reserve

Like active-duty Airmen, reserve Airmen in the survey were mostly male, enlisted, and married, with one or two children.[27] However, they were also slightly older, with more than half of them over the age of 35, and had more experience in the Air Force. Roughly 5 percent had a family member with a special need. All reserve Airmen in the sample lived off base, and roughly two-thirds lived within 50 miles of their base assignments.[28] Finally, like their active-duty peers, reserve Airmen rated themselves very highly on both the self-rated coping scale and the CD-RISC 2.

Outcomes and Results from Multilevel Models

We explore a wide range of outcomes in the Community Assessment Survey that could be linked to an Airman's base area. We group our outcome variables into five categories: health and well-being; social support, integration, and cohesion; neighborhood resources; satisfaction; and career. We first present the distribution of each outcome, by group, for four different groups of Airmen: all active-duty Airmen, active-duty Airmen who lived on base, active-duty Airmen who lived off base, and all reserve Airmen in our analytic sample. We then turn to the results from the multilevel models linking Airman outcomes to the RAND BASE-I and its domains.

In the sections that follow, we discuss only significant results from the full model (i.e., the model that includes control variables). For active-duty Airmen, the control variables include gender, age, marital status, dual military couple, number of children, Exceptional Family Member Program (EFMP) or Special Needs Identification Assignment Coordination (SNIAC) family member, rank, years of service, currently deployed, time at current base, distance from current base, self-rated coping, and the CD-RISC 2. Control variables for reserve Airmen are the same except for time at current base, which was not available in the survey data. All control variables occur at the individual level. That is, no base-level control variables (e.g., region, population density) are included. A summary of all the results from the Community Assessment Survey can be found in Table D.5 in Appendix D.

---

[27] A detailed table of demographic statistics for reserve Airmen in the analytic sample can be found in Table D.4 in Appendix D.

[28] Note that not all reserve Airmen included in our analytic sample were assigned to a major Air Force installation with more than 1,000 permanent party military personnel; this was one of our criteria for installation selection for this study. Reserve Airmen assigned to smaller guard and reserve bases were excluded from our analysis.

Before presenting the results, it is important to acknowledge that *statistical significance* is not always synonymous with *practical significance*. One measure of practical significance is an effect size. Effect sizes represent a way to gauge the magnitude of an association—in this case, between the RAND BASE-I and its constituent domains and Airman outcomes. It is possible that, although the RAND BASE-I or a domain has a statistically significant association with an outcome, that association may have a small effect size. However, certain factors make interpreting effect sizes a bit more complex in the context of neighborhood studies.

First, it is not clear where to draw a cutoff of importance among the calculated effect sizes (e.g., is 0.05 meaningful? What about 0.03?). Second, we expected the impact of base-area factors to be small, given that so many other variables are likely to be associated with the outcomes we examined. The effect sizes are not outside the range that we would have expected for this type of analysis. However, small effect sizes do suggest that other factors are likely more strongly associated with outcomes. Third, there is no gold standard for calculating effect sizes in multilevel analyses. We have opted for one method (standardizing at the individual level versus the base level), but others are also possible. For these reasons, we have opted to focus on statistical significance in the main body of the report but do offer effect sizes in appendix tables (see Tables D.6 and D.7 in Appendix D).

Ultimately, when interpreting the results, one must always remember that neighborhood characteristics do not operate in a vacuum. That is, other factors, at the individual Airman, family, and base levels, are all associated with outcomes. We reiterate that the results we present should not be viewed as causal. Rather, significant associations, and their effect sizes, give some indication of the strength of the relationship between base-area characteristics and outcomes at the level of individual Airmen.

Health and Well-Being

We include three outcomes related to health and well-being: exercise frequency, self-rated health, and depressive symptoms. Table 4.1 shows the distribution of these outcomes across the four groups of Airmen.

Table 4.1

Health and Well-Being Outcomes from the Community Assessment Survey, by Group

Outcome	Total Active Duty	On Base	Off Base	Reserve
Exercise frequency (in past month)[a]	5.3 (1.6)	5.4 (1.6)	5.2 (1.6)	4.8 (1.7)
Self-rated health[b]	4.3 (1.0)	4.3 (1.0)	4.3 (1.0)	4.4 (1.0)
Depressive symptoms (in past week)[c]	9.9 (3.7)	10.0 (3.8)	9.8 (3.6)	9.3 (3.2)

[a] Possible range from "never" (1) to "every day" (9).
[b] Possible range from "very poor" (1) to "excellent" (6).
[c] Mean of seven items, possible range from "none" (1) to "5–7 days" (4). Scores range from 7 to 28.
NOTE: The table presents mean values. Numbers in parentheses are standard deviations (SDs).

Exercise Frequency

Physical fitness and exercise frequency are measured by one item asking Airmen to indicate how often they had exercised in the past month. We use a continuous outcome that ranges from never to every day. Interval answer options are mostly measured weekly (e.g., once a week, twice a week). On average, active-duty Airmen reported exercising three days per week (score of 5.3; see Table 4.1). Perhaps not surprisingly, reserve Airmen reported exercising at a somewhat lower weekly frequency (score of 4.8, or somewhere between twice and three times per week). We expected that higher-scoring base areas on the RAND BASE-I may have more recreation opportunities and thus that Airmen who lived there may exercise at a greater frequency.

The multilevel models revealed no significant association for exercise frequency in the full model with control variables. The full model for the housing domain is negative and statistically significant: Airmen who lived in areas that score high on the housing domain reported lower frequency of exercise. Recall that each domain is entered into the model alone, so domain-specific models *do not* control for the other five domains.

Self-Rated Health

Self-rated health is measured by one item: "How would you rate your health during the past four weeks?" Answers range from "very poor" (1) to "excellent" (6). This question is standard in most surveys of health and well-being. Active-duty and reserve Airmen rated their health somewhere between "good" and "very good" (active duty: 4.3; reserve: 4.4; see Table 4.1). We expected that RAND BASE-I ratings would be positively associated with self-rated health—that is, that Airmen who lived in higher-quality base areas would rate their health as better than those who lived in lower-quality areas.

The overall RAND BASE-I was not associated with self-rated health. One domain, household composition, was significantly and negatively associated with self-rated health.

Depressive Symptoms

A modified version of the Center for Epidemiologic Studies Depression Scale (CES-D) (Radloff, 1977) was used to assess depressive symptoms.[29] Items asked respondents about the frequency with which they had experienced seven symptoms: felt that they just could not get going, felt sad, had trouble getting to sleep or staying asleep, felt that everything was an effort, felt lonely, felt that they could not shake the blues, and had trouble keeping their minds on what they were doing. Respondents could experience these symptoms never or, out of the past seven days or week, one to two days, three to four days, or five to seven days. This means that scores on the depressive-symptom measure range from 7, which indicates no symptoms on any day, to 28, which indicates all symptoms being experienced almost every day. Airmen in our analytic sample had a score of roughly 10 on the depressive-symptom scale, with little variation (SD = 4). To put this in context, someone who reported experiencing a single symptom (e.g., "feeling like they couldn't get going") three to four out of the previous four days would receive a score of 3. Thus, to receive a score of 9, someone would have to endorse at least three symptoms three or four days out of the past week (or fewer symptoms at a longer duration or more symptoms at a shorter duration). We expected that individuals who lived in higher-ranked base areas would report, on average, fewer depressive symptoms.

The multilevel models yielded three significant associations for depressive symptoms, all among active-duty Airmen. Active-duty Airmen who lived in base areas characterized by higher scores on the household composition domain, the employment domain, and the transportation domain all reported more depressive symptoms than their peers who lived in base areas with lower scores on these domains. However, it is not clear why living in an area with higher employment (and lower unemployment), fewer female-headed households, smaller households, and shorter commute times would be associated with more depressive symptoms.

Social Support, Integration, and Cohesion

The second category of outcomes from the Community Assessment Survey includes measures related to the social support, integration, and cohesion of the neighborhoods

---

[29] Because the CES-D was not intended to be a diagnostic measure, there is no clinical cutoff that defines major depression or any other depressive disorder.

where Airmen and their families live. Sometimes, these measures referred to the Air Force community itself (i.e., the installation or base). Other times, the measures simply asked about the Airman's "community." Generally, these measures are not considered traditional indicators of health and well-being; however, they may positively (or negatively) affect such indicators. For example, some research has found that individuals who live in areas with higher levels of social capital (i.e., trust between citizens, norms of reciprocity, group membership, capacity for collective action) and social cohesion report better self-rated health (Echeverría et al., 2008; Kawachi, Kennedy, and Glass, 1999; D. Kim et al., 2010). We include seven measures in this outcome category: base social cohesion, neighborhood social cohesion, an Airman community engagement scale, neighborhood social support, community safety, child safety, and support for youth. Table 4.2 shows the distribution of these outcomes across the four groups of Airmen.

Table 4.2
Social Support, Integration, and Cohesion Outcomes from the Community Assessment Survey, by Group

Outcome	Total Active Duty	On Base	Off Base	Reserve
Base social cohesion[a]	4.0 (1.2)	4.1 (1.2)	3.9 (1.2)	N/A
Neighborhood social cohesion[a]	3.8 (1.4)	3.8 (1.4)	3.8 (1.4)	4.3 (1.2)
Airman community engagement scale[a]	4.2 (1.1)	4.3 (1.1)	4.1 (1.0)	4.1 (1.2)
Neighborhood social support[b]	4.2 (1.6)	4.2 (1.5)	4.2 (1.6)	4.3 (1.5)
Community safety[c]	5.1 (0.9)	5.4 (0.9)	5.1 (0.9)	5.3 (0.8)
Child safety[d]	5.0 (1.0)	5.0 (1.0)	5.0 (0.9)	5.2 (0.9)
Support for youth[e]	4.2 (1.1)	4.2 (1.1)	4.2 (1.1)	N/A

[a] Mean of four items, possible range "strongly disagree" (1) to "strongly agree" (6).
[b] Mean of four items, possible range "almost never" (1) to "almost always" (6).
[c] One item, possible range "very unsafe" (1) to "very safe" (6).
[d] Mean of two items, possible range "almost never" (1) to "almost always" (6). Recoded so that higher scores indicate greater perception of child safety.
[e] Mean of two items, possible range "strongly disagree" (1) to "strongly agree" (5).
NOTE: The table presents mean values. Numbers in parentheses are standard deviations. N/A = Not applicable.

Base Social Cohesion

Four survey items asked Airmen to assess the community climate among fellow Airmen and families assigned to their same bases (these items were asked only of active-duty Airmen). Airmen were asked to agree or disagree (on a six-point scale) with the following statements: Members and families assigned to this base "feel a sense of common mission and purpose," "show teamwork and cooperation," "feel a collective sense of community," and "feel connected to other members and families." These four items assessed the social cohesion, or social connectedness, of the base and its members. They were rated on a scale from "strongly disagree" (1) to "strongly agree" (6). Overall, active-duty Airmen agreed that social cohesion on their bases was moderate, with average score of 4 (which corresponds to "slightly agree"; see Table 4.2). We might expect that Airmen assigned to bases with higher scores on the RAND BASE-I would also have higher scores on the base social cohesion scale if the base and community were well integrated. However, if the surrounding community were high quality and not well integrated with the base, Airmen and their families might be less likely to spend time on base, socializing and forging relationships with other Air Force personnel. In the latter case, we would expect high RAND BASE-I scores to be associated with lower base cohesion scores.

According to the multilevel models, active-duty Airmen who lived in higher-quality base areas (as ranked by the overall RAND BASE-I) reported lower base social cohesion. The same is true for Airmen whose base areas scored higher in the household composition domain, the employment domain, the income and poverty domain, the housing domain, and the social domain.

Neighborhood Social Cohesion

Similar to base social cohesion, the measure of neighborhood social cohesion attempts to measure social connectedness, except that, in this case, the survey items apply to the Airman's neighborhood. The survey did not define *neighborhood* for Airmen but rather allowed them to interpret what *neighborhood* meant to them (e.g., it could be the block on which the Airman lived, the section of the city or town in which he or she lived, the base neighborhood). Three items assess neighborhood social cohesion: People in my neighborhood "know the names of their neighbors, look out for one another," "offer help or assistance to one another in times of need," and "talk to or visit with neighbors." Responses ranged from "strongly disagree" (1) to "strongly agree" (6). Overall, active-duty Airmen agreed that social cohesion on their bases was moderate, with an average score of 3.8 (which corresponds to "slightly agree"; see Table 4.2). Reserve Airmen showed slightly greater support for the neighborhood social cohesion items, with a mean of 4.3. From prior research of civilians, we expected that Airmen assigned to bases with higher scores on the RAND BASE-I would also have higher scores on the neighborhood social cohesion scale.

Among active-duty Airmen, overall quality of the base areas had no significant association with neighborhood social cohesion. But the income and poverty domain showed a significant association, in which lower neighborhood social cohesion was reported among Airmen who lived in areas where income was high and poverty rates were low. Airmen who lived off base rated the social cohesion of their neighborhoods even more negatively than their on-base peers did.

Among reserve Airmen, however, the overall RAND BASE-I is significantly associated with ratings of neighborhood social cohesion: Contrary to our hypothesis, living in a higher-quality base area is associated with lower neighborhood social cohesion. This negative association is especially true for the social domain. The housing and transportation domains are actually positively associated with neighborhood social cohesion. So reserve Airmen who lived in areas where residents spend a smaller percentage of their income on housing and there are lower residential turnover and shorter commute times to work said that the social cohesion in their neighborhoods was higher than Airmen living in areas characterized by residents who spend more of their income on housing and there are greater residential turnover and longer commute times.

Airman Community Engagement Scale

Community capacity is assessed by Airmen's agreement with four statements: "Active duty/Reserve members are active in base-sponsored community events and activities," "assume responsibility for making this base a better place to live and work," "join together to solve problems that threaten the safety and well-being of members and families assigned to this base," and "take advantage of opportunities to address the support needs of members and families assigned to this base." All items were measured on a six-point scale, from "very dissatisfied" (1) to "very satisfied" (6). These items also attempt to measure aspects of social cohesion but focus on the ability to make things happen with respect to health and well-being of Airmen and their families. So they can be thought of as the base community's capacity for collective action. Both active-duty and reserve Airmen reported slight agreement (corresponding to a score of 4) with the Airman community engagement items. This suggests a moderate, but not high, level of Airman community engagement in the base areas where these Airmen lived. We expected that Airmen living in base areas that score higher on the overall RAND BASE-I would also have higher ratings on the Airman community engagement scale.

Among both active-duty and reserve Airmen, the overall RAND BASE-I is negatively associated with Airman community engagement. That is, in higher-quality base areas, Airmen had a lower degree of satisfaction with their fellow Airmen's ability to work together and act collectively to promote and improve life on base. We found similar results for the household composition domain, the employment domain (reserve only), the income and poverty domain, and the housing domain (reserve only). If Airmen who lived in base areas that score high on the RAND BASE-I spend more nonworking time involved in their off-base community than on base, then they may not be able to develop the sense of community among Airmen.

We also found that reserve Airmen who lived in base areas with higher scores on the transportation domain (i.e., shorter commute times and greater access to an automobile) reported greater engagement in the Air Force community. Given that reserve Airmen do not have to live near their assigned base, it is not clear why a shorter commute time to work would be associated with greater involvement in the base community.

Neighborhood Social Support

Four items measure Airmen's perception of the support provided by their community. The neighborhood support scale is the mean of the following items: At your current location, are there friends, neighbors, co-workers, or relatives outside your home who would "lend you household tools or equipment, provide transportation if you needed it," "give you information about available community agencies and resources," and "take care of your child(ren) in an emergency (if applicable)." Responses ranged from "almost never" (1) to "almost always" (6). Both active-duty and reserve Airmen gave an average response of 4, corresponding to "about half of the time" (see Table 4.2). We expected that perceptions of neighborhood support would be greater in base areas that score higher on the overall RAND BASE-I and were especially curious about the social domain, which contains a measure of military veterans in the base area.

We found only one significant association for neighborhood support in the multilevel models. Airmen who lived in base areas with residents who have shorter commute times to work and greater access to automobiles were more likely to perceive their neighborhoods to have more support. Perhaps the shorter commute times and greater access to vehicles allow residents to spend more time in their neighborhoods interacting with others, building a sense of social cohesion and the perception that neighbors would look out for each other.

Community Safety

Community safety is measured by one item asking Airmen, "In general, how safe are you from crime and violence in your neighborhood?" Response categories ranged from "very unsafe" (1) to "very safe" (6). Overall, both active-duty and reserve Airmen rated their communities as safe (active duty: 5.1; reserve: 5.3; see Table 4.2). We expected that Airmen who were assigned to higher-scoring base areas, both on the RAND BASE-I and on the domains, would rate community safety higher than those in lower-scoring base areas.

Among active-duty Airmen, the overall RAND BASE-I was positively associated with perceptions of community safety. That is, Airmen who lived in higher-quality base areas rated them as safer.[30] The same was true for the household composition domain, the employment domain, the housing domain, and the social domain. Here we also see evidence of an exposure effect because safety ratings were even higher among active-duty Airmen who live off versus on base. Only the housing domain had a significant and positive association with perceptions of safety among reserve Airmen.

Child Safety

The perceived safety of children is assessed by two survey items asked only of parents with school-age children: "How often are you afraid that someone will hurt or bother your child(ren) at school?" and "How often are you afraid that someone will hurt or bother your child(ren) on the way to or from school?" Responses to categories ranged from "almost never" (1) to "almost always" (6) and were reverse-coded so that higher scores indicated greater perception of safety. Both active-duty and reserve Airmen rated the safety of their children as high; the average score was just over 5, which, when reverse-coded, translates into a rating of "rarely" (active duty: 5.0; reserve: 5.2; see Table 4.2). We expected that Airmen who were assigned to higher-scoring base areas, both on the RAND BASE-I and on the domains, would rate safety of children in the areas higher than those in lower-scoring base areas.

Among active-duty Airmen, only the housing domain was associated with perceived safety of children: Airmen who lived in base areas characterized by more affordable housing for residents and less residential turnover rated child safety higher. It is possible that this domain is picking up on aspects of neighborhood cohesion. We found no significant associations for reserve Airmen.

Support for Youth

Two items asked only active-duty parents about community support for youth (specified as those between the ages of 10 and 18). Parents rated how in agreement they were with the following statements: Youth who are sons and daughters of active-duty service members assigned to the Air Force installation "are supported and valued by base

---

[30] The finding that higher-quality (especially as characterized by higher SES and informal social control and lower social disorganization) neighborhoods are generally safer (i.e., have less crime) than lower-quality neighborhoods is also supported in the civilian literature (for examples, see Bellair and Browning, 2010; Hipp, 2010; and Sampson, Morenoff, and Gannon-Rowley, 2002).

leadership" and "have opportunities for interesting and meaningful uses of their time." Responses ranged from "strongly disagree" (1) to "strongly agree" (6). Active-duty Airmen reported slight agreement with the support for youth items (score of 4.2), indicating that they were not completely satisfied with the support their children received from the base and base leadership (see Table 4.2). We expected more support for these items from Airmen who lived in higher-scoring base areas. However, our multilevel models revealed no significant associations between the RAND BASE-I or the six domains and perceptions of support for youth among either active-duty or reserve Airmen.

Neighborhood Resources

The Community Assessment Survey contained some questions that tapped into the resources available to Airmen and their families. These measures were subjective in that Airmen were asked to rate availability or quality of resources in their communities. Thus, they provide a good test of whether the objective index of area quality that we have created is reflected by Airmen's subjective ratings of community resources. This outcome group includes five measures: a community resource scale (including subscales for housing, health care, child care, job, transportation, and child activities), school quality, child-care spending, an economic stress scale, and financial stress. Table 4.3 shows the distribution of these outcomes across the four groups of Airmen.

Table 4.3

Neighborhood Resource Outcomes from the Community Assessment Survey, by Group

Outcome	Total Active Duty	On Base	Off Base	Reserve
Community resource scale				
Overall[a]	4.7 (1.0)	4.7 (1.2)	4.7 (1.2)	N/A
Housing subscale[b]	4.6 (1.5)	4.4 (1.4)	4.7 (1.5)	N/A
Health care subscale[b]	4.5 (1.4)	4.5 (1.4)	4.5 (1.4)	N/A
Child-care subscale[c]	5.4 (1.7)	5.4 (1.8)	5.4 (1.7)	N/A
Job subscale[d]	4.5 (2.1)	4.3 (2.1)	4.6 (2.1)	N/A
Transportation subscale[d]	4.6 (2.1)	4.5 (2.2)	4.7 (2.1)	N/A
Child activity subscale[d]	4.7 (1.6)	4.5 (1.6)	4.8 (1.5)	N/A
School quality[b]	4.6 (1.2)	4.4 (1.3)	4.7 (1.2)	5.0 (1.0)
Child-care spending (per week)[e]	4.1 (1.4)	4.0 (1.3)	4.2 (1.4)	3.8 (1.5)
Economic stress scale[f]	1.6 (0.8)	1.6 (0.8)	1.5 (0.8)	1.7 (0.9)
Financial stress[g]	N/A	N/A	N/A	2.0 (1.01)

[a] Mean of 11 items, possible range "very dissatisfied" (1) to "very satisfied" (6).
[b] Mean of two items, possible range "very dissatisfied" (1) to "very satisfied" (6). Asked only of those who have children and report using child care.
[c] Mean of four items, possible range "very dissatisfied" (1) to "very satisfied" (6).
[d] Mean of one item, possible range "very dissatisfied" (1) to "very satisfied" (6).
[e] Possible range "$50 or less" (1) to "more than $250" (6).
[f] Mean of two items, possible range "no difficulty at all" (1) to "a great deal of difficulty" (5).
[g] Mean of four items, possible range "strongly disagree" (1) to "strongly agree" (6).
NOTE: The table presents mean values. Numbers in parentheses are standard deviations.

Community Resource Scale

Active-duty Airmen were asked about their satisfaction with 11 aspects of the area to which they were assigned or where they lived, including both on- and off-base resources: availability of housing, quality of housing, availability of health care, quality of health care, availability of weekly child care (if applicable), quality of weekly child care (if applicable), affordability of weekly child care (if applicable), availability of hourly child care (if applicable), job opportunities for civilian spouses (if applicable), availability of public transportation, and availability of activities for children and youth (if applicable).

Response categories ranged from "very dissatisfied" (1) to "very satisfied" (6). Overall, active-duty Airmen reported being somewhere between "slightly satisfied" and "satisfied" with the resources available to them in their communities (score of 4.7; see Table 4.3). One would expect that these types of community resources would be more plentiful in areas with higher SES. We thus expected that Airmen assigned to base areas with higher scores on the RAND BASE-I, especially the income and poverty domain, would be more satisfied with the availability of overall community resources.

We also include six subscales of the overall community resource scale: housing, health care, child care, jobs, transportation, and child activities. Satisfaction with quality, availability, and affordability with child care was the highest (5.4), while satisfaction with the quality and availability of health care was the lowest (4.5). Although these subscales are also likely associated with overall RAND BASE-I scores, we also wanted to assess their associations with individual domains. For example, we expected that satisfaction with the availability of public transportation would be positively associated with both the income and poverty domain and the transportation domain. The job subscale should also be positively associated with the employment domain.

We focus our discussion on the overall community resource scale because results for the subscales are similar (see Table D.5 in Appendix D). Among active-duty Airmen, the overall RAND BASE-I is positively associated with satisfaction with community resources. And this association is strong among Airmen who lived off base. So, in higher-quality base areas, Airmen were more satisfied with the resources available to them (e.g., child care, health care, public transportation). This again provides evidence that our objective index is tapping into an underlying measure of the quality of community resources that Airmen perceive subjectively.

We also found that the income and poverty domain, the housing domain, and the social domain are also positively associated with community resource satisfaction. Again, this is not surprising given that these domains are largely reflective of the SES of a base area. And these associations are stronger for Airmen who lived off base, supporting our exposure hypothesis that Airmen who live off base are more "affected" by the characteristics of their communities, presumably because they spend more time there than their on-base peers do. The transportation domain is actually negatively associated with community resource satisfaction. This is consistent with other findings from our analysis that suggest that the areas where shorter commute times are found may be more rural. These results suggest that these same areas may also have fewer resources for the Airmen who live there.

School Quality

Two items assess subjective school quality, as rated by Airmen with school-age children: "Overall, how satisfied are you with the quality of the schools your children attend?" and "How satisfied are you with the education option for your children this school year?" Response categories ranged from "very dissatisfied" (1) to "very satisfied" (6). Active-duty Airmen were "slightly satisfied" with school quality (score of 4.6), with reserve Airmen indicating a slightly higher level of satisfaction (score of 5.0) (see Table 4.3). We expected that Airmen in areas with higher-scoring base areas would rate school quality as higher.

For both active-duty and reserve Airmen, living in a base area with a higher rating on the RAND BASE-I is associated with a higher subjective rating of school quality. The same is true for the household composition domain, the employment domain, the income and poverty domain, the housing domain, and the social domain. These results suggest that base areas characterized by higher SES (e.g., lower unemployment rates, lower poverty rates, higher incomes, more highly educated residents, more married families) have higher-quality schools (see Aikens and Barbarin, 2008). For active-duty Airmen, those who lived off base rated the quality of schools higher than did their on-base peers. This supports our exposure hypothesis that Airmen who live off base, who presumably spend more time in their civilian communities, are more "exposed" to area factors and thus show stronger associations between the RAND BASE-I and domains than their peers who live on base.

Child-Care Spending

Of those parents who use child care on a weekly basis, the survey asked what amount of money was spent on that service. Active-duty Airmen reported spending between $101 and $150 per week, on average, on child care (see Table 4.3). Among reserve Airmen, the expense was slightly less, between $76 and $100 per week. Although it is not entirely clear what to expect in terms of the association between the RAND BASE-I and spending on child care, we believed that higher-quality base areas would have more-affordable options for child care and, thus, predicted a negative association between the two (i.e., higher RAND BASE-I scores will be associated with lower child-care costs). However, it is also possible that individuals who live in higher-quality areas can afford more-expensive quality and are willing to pay for such care. This would lead to a positive association between the RAND BASE-I and spending on child care.

According to the multilevel model results, active-duty Airmen who lived in base areas with higher scores on the overall RAND BASE-I spent more on their child care. It is likely that Airmen who can afford to live in higher-quality areas also choose to pay more for the convenience of off-base child care near their homes or fall on the higher end of the sliding-scale fee structure for on-base child care. Of course, it is also possible that high-quality and affordable child care is lacking in these areas. Although we cannot tease these possibilities apart, we do know from the survey items on community resources that the highest satisfaction levels were reported for quality, availability, and affordability with child care.

We find a similar positive association with child-care spending for the household composition domain, the employment domain, the income and poverty domain, and the social domain. Those who live in high-quality areas tend to purchase more-expensive child care.

Economic Stress Scale

Two items from the survey form an economic stress scale. Respondents rated how much difficulty they had "living on your total income right now" and "paying your bills each month." Response categories ranged from "no difficulty at all" (1) to "a great deal of difficulty" (5), so higher scores indicate more stress. Both active-duty and reserve Airmen reported having somewhere between "no difficulty at all" and "a little difficulty" when it comes to finances (active duty: 1.6; reserve: 1.7; see Table 4.3). Although living in a higher-scoring base area is generally thought to be associated with positive outcomes, in this case, it may contribute to a negative outcome (i.e., more financial difficulty). If Airmen are assigned to higher-quality areas but do not have the means to comfortably live in those areas, they may experience a higher degree of financial stress.

Among active-duty Airmen, the overall RAND BASE-I was negatively associated with economic stress. So, in base areas with higher RAND BASE-I scores, Airmen reported fewer problems with finances. The same was true for the income and poverty and social domains. Interestingly, the transportation domain is positively associated with economic stress. As we noted above, areas with the shortest commute times are generally in more-rural areas. Perhaps financial compensation at these bases is not great enough and it is in these areas that families may find it harder to make ends meet. However, we caution that the mean level of difficulty across the entire sample was somewhere between having no difficulty and having "a little" difficulty. So, although some families are clearly under very significant economic stress, most are not. None of the associations was significant for reserve Airmen.[31]

---

[31] However, see the results below for financial stress among reserve Airmen only.

Financial Stress

Four items assess financial stress among reserve Airmen. Airmen rated how much they agreed with the following statements: "I have lost a significant level of income because of my Reserve duties," "I have used personal or family savings to meet financial obligations because of my Reserve duties," "I have borrowed money or taken a loan in order to meet my financial obligations because of my Reserve duties," and "I have incurred substantial debt because of my Reserve duties." Response categories ranged from "strongly disagree" (1) to "strongly agree" (6). On average, reserve Airmen disagreed that their reserve duties had caused them financial difficulties (score of 2.0; see Table 4.3). Similar to what we find for the economic distress measure for active-duty Airmen, we hypothesized that financial stress may actually be greater for Airmen who lived in higher-quality base areas. However, multilevel model results indicated no significant association between the RAND BASE-I and financial stress. Given the low level of stress reported by reserve Airmen, this is perhaps not surprising. The social domain is, however, significantly and negatively associated with financial stress. This finding is also perhaps not surprising given that the social domain captures the average education level of the base area.

Satisfaction

We include three satisfaction items in order to assess whether community resources, quality, and characteristics are associated with the RAND BASE-I and its constituent domains: satisfaction with base assignment, satisfaction with the Air Force way of life, and community satisfaction. Table 4.4 shows the distribution of these outcomes across the four groups of Airmen.

Table 4.4
Satisfaction Outcomes from the Community Assessment Survey, by Group

Outcome	Total Active Duty	On Base	Off Base	Reserve
Base assignment	4.1 (1.6)	3.9 (1.6)	4.2 (1.5)	4.8 (1.2)
Air Force way of life	4.4 (1.3)	4.5 (1.3)	4.4 (1.3)	4.6 (1.3)
Community	3.6 (1.4)	3.3 (1.4)	3.7 (1.3)	4.1 (1.2)

NOTE: The table presents mean values. Numbers in parentheses are standard deviations. Possible range "very dissatisfied" (1) to "very satisfied" (6) or "very poor" (1) to "excellent" (6).

Satisfaction with Base Assignment

All Airmen were asked how satisfied they were with their assignment to their current bases on a six-point scale, from "very dissatisfied" (1) to "very satisfied" (6). Active-duty Airmen indicated that they were "slightly satisfied" (a score of 4.1) with their base assignments, with those living on base reporting slightly lower satisfaction levels (see Table 4.4). Reserve Airmen reported higher satisfaction with base assignment than their active-duty peers (a score of 4.8). Airmen assigned to bases with higher ratings on the overall RAND BASE-I should have a higher satisfaction level with their current base assignments.

For reserve Airmen, the overall RAND BASE-I was positively associated with base assignment satisfaction. So living in a higher-quality area was associated with greater satisfaction with being assigned to the current base. This was not true for active-duty Airmen. For both active-duty and reserve Airmen, living in base areas with higher scores on the social domain was associated with greater satisfaction with base assignment. So in areas with a more highly educated population, a larger percentage of married families, and a larger military veteran population, Airmen were more positive about their own base assignments. However, among active-duty Airmen, those who lived in base areas with shorter commute times and greater access to automobiles were actually less satisfied with their base assignments. If shorter commute times are correlated with very rural areas, then this result may suggest that Airmen are less satisfied with living in remote areas of the country. And in fact, of the top ten base areas with the shortest commute times, all ten are located in states with large rural areas, such as North Dakota (e.g., Minot, Grand Forks), South Dakota (e.g., Ellsworth), Oklahoma (e.g., Altus, Vance), Montana (e.g., Malmstrom), Arkansas (e.g., Eielson), New Mexico (e.g., Cannon), and Texas (e.g., Dyess, Sheppard). Many AFBs are situated in areas where large amounts of unoccupied land are available. These areas tend to be rural.

Satisfaction with the Air Force Way of Life

As they were for satisfaction with base assignment, Airmen were also asked to rate their satisfaction with the "Air Force/Air Force Reserve way of life," on a six-point scale, from "very dissatisfied" (1) to "very satisfied" (6). Both active-duty and reserve Airmen reported being "slightly satisfied" with the Air Force way of life (active duty: 4.4; reserve: 4.6; see Table 4.4). We expected that Airmen who were assigned to bases with higher ratings on the overall RAND BASE-I would also have higher levels of satisfaction with the Air Force way of life.

Among active-duty Airmen, living in a base area with a higher score on the household composition domain or a higher score on the transportation domain (also among reserve Airmen) is associated with lower satisfaction with the Air Force way of life. And satisfaction scores were even lower among those Airmen who lived off base.[32] Again, it is possible that shorter commute times are concentrated in less urban areas, leading to general dissatisfaction with the Air Force. Higher scores on the social domain are associated with higher satisfaction scores. So Airmen living in areas with a more highly educated population, more married families, and more military veterans were also more satisfied with their Air Force experience.

Satisfaction with Community

The final satisfaction question we examine is overall satisfaction with one's community. This question asked, "Overall, how would you rate the local area in which your base is located as a place to live," on a six-point scale, from "very dissatisfied" (1) to "very satisfied" (6). Active-duty Airmen reported being somewhere between "slightly dissatisfied" and "slightly satisfied" with their communities (score of 3.6), with Airmen living on base being somewhat less satisfied than their off-base peers. Reserve Airmen reported being "slightly satisfied" with their communities (score of 4.1) (see Table 4.4). Informed by our findings for the other satisfaction items, we expected that Airmen who were assigned to bases with higher ratings on the overall RAND BASE-I would also have higher levels of satisfaction with the surrounding community.

According to our multilevel models, among both active-duty and reserve Airmen, higher scores on the overall RAND BASE-I are associated with greater community satisfaction. In some sense, this is a "test" of our objective index because it suggests that the census data we used to construct the measure of base-area quality do map onto individual, subjective ratings of where people live. So, in higher-quality base areas, as measured by the RAND BASE-I, Airmen rated the subjective quality of their areas to be higher as well.

Scores on the household domain, the income and poverty domain, the housing domain, and the social domain are also positively associated with community satisfaction. These are areas characterized by fewer single-parent households, smaller household sizes, higher income, lower poverty rates, more affordable housing, lower residential turnover, more highly educated populations, more married families, and more military veterans. The employment domain was also important for reserve Airmen, which is perhaps not surprising given that they are not employed full time by the Air Force. So these Airmen were more satisfied with their communities when the base area experienced higher employment and lower unemployment.

---

[32] The opposite is true for reserve Airmen, for whom higher scores on the transportation domain are actually associated with higher satisfaction levels.

Career

The final set of outcomes we examine is those related to Airmen's careers. For active-duty and reserve Airmen, the Community Assessment Survey asked whether the Airman planned on staying in the Air Force until eligible for retirement (generally 20 years of service). Reserve Airmen were also asked about their perceptions of employer support both in general and during a period of deployment. Table 4.5 shows the distribution of these outcomes across the four groups of Airmen.

Table 4.5
Career Outcomes from the Community Assessment Survey, by Group

Outcome	Total Active Duty	On Base	Off Base	Reserve
Career intentions[a]	0.6	0.6	0.6	0.8
	(0.5)	(0.5)	(0.5)	(0.4)
Employer support[b]	N/A	N/A	N/A	4.8
				(1.2)
Employer support during deployment[c]	N/A	N/A	N/A	2.8
				(1.6)

[a] Remain in Air Force until retirement; possible values: 1 = yes, 0 = no.
[b] Mean of two items, possible range "strongly disagree" (1) to "strongly agree" (5).
[c] Mean of two items, possible range from "very great extent" (1) to "no extent" (6). Asked only of Airmen who have been deployed in the past 12 months. Recoded so that higher scores indicate greater perceived support.
NOTE: The table presents mean values. Numbers in parentheses are standard deviations. N/A = not applicable.

Career Intentions

We were specifically interested in whether or not Airmen indicated that they were planning on staying in the military until retirement (or 20 years of service). Roughly 60 percent of active-duty and 77 percent of reserve Airmen indicated that they planned on staying in the military until they were eligible for full retirement benefits (see Table 4.5). Of course, we must keep in mind that career intentions are not always perfectly correlated with actual retention behavior, despite being a good predictor of such behavior (see Guthrie, 1992; Marsh, 1989; Janega and Olmsted, 2003; Jans and Frazer-Jans, 2006). We explored whether Airmen currently assigned to base areas that score higher on the overall RAND BASE-I would be more satisfied with their life in the Air Force and thus more likely to endorse the Air Force as a career. Using our multilevel models, we did not find a significant association between the RAND BASE-I and career intentions.

Employer Support

Reserve Airmen were asked how much they disagree with two statements about their current employers (these items were asked only of those who had a job): "My civilian employer understands my Air Force duty responsibilities" and "My civilian employer tries to help me meet my Air Force duty responsibilities." Response categories ranged from "strongly disagree" (1) to "strongly agree" (6). Overall, reserve Airmen slightly agreed that their employers were supportive (score of 4.8; see Table 4.5). Although we did expect that the overall RAND BASE-I would be positively associated with employer support (i.e., Airmen who lived in higher-quality base areas would report more employer support), the social domain is of particular interest because it contains information about the percentage of the civilian population who are military veterans. If employers are veterans, or if employers have had positive experiences hiring veterans (or current military), then they may be more supportive. Thus we also expected the social domain to be positively associated with employer support.

Employer Support During Deployment

The Community Assessment Survey also included two items about employer support during deployment: "Was your employer supportive to you while you were deployed?" and "Is your employer supportive of you remaining in the Reserves?" These items were asked only of Airmen who had been deployed in the past 12 months. Response categories ranged from "very great extent" (1) to "no extent" (6). Scores are reverse-coded so that higher scores indicate greater perceptions of employer support during deployment. Airmen felt less supported by employers during deployment, reporting that they either disagreed or slightly disagreed with the two survey items (score of 2.8; see Table 4.5). Informed by what we found for general employer support, we expected employer support during deployment to be positively associated with the overall RAND BASE-I, as well as the social domain.

The overall RAND BASE-I is negatively associated with perceived employer support. So, in higher-quality base areas, reserve Airmen actually perceived lower levels of support from their employers. The same was true for the employment domain and the income and poverty domain. It could be that, in areas where employment is strong, employers do not need to rely as heavily on employees whom they know may need to take long leaves of absence to fulfill their reserve duties. If other workers are able to pick up any slack that may result from their absence, perhaps reserve Airmen do not perceive any special attention from their employers, relative to what other employees may receive. In fact, civilian employees may be given more support because they may eventually have to do more in their coworkers' absences. We found no significant associations for support during deployment. Given that reserve Airmen, on average, reported very little support from their employers during periods of deployment, we are not surprised by this result.

Discussion

In this chapter, we presented results from multilevel models linking the RAND BASE-I and its six constituent domains to various measures of the well-being of Airmen and their families.[33] Overall, we find some evidence that RAND BASE-I scores are correlated with different aspects of community satisfaction, satisfaction with resources, and aspects of neighborhood social cohesion (see Figure 4.1 and Table 4.6). However, we cannot definitely determine whether these associations are causal.

Figure 4.1
Summary of Results for Overall RAND Base Area Social and Economic Index for the Community Assessment Survey, by Group

Base areas with higher RAND BASE-I scores	
Active Duty	**Reserve**
√ Report lower levels of base social cohesion.	√ Report greater satisfaction with base assignment.
√ Report higher satisfaction with community resources, including health care, child care, jobs, public transportation and child activities.	√ Report higher community satisfaction.
√ Report lower economic stress.	√ Report lower Airman community engagement.
√ Report higher community satisfaction.	√ Report lower neighborhood social cohesion.
√ Perceive greater community safety.	√ Perceive higher school quality.
√ Perceive higher school quality.	√ Report less support from employers.
√ Spend more on child care.	
√ Rate Airman community engagement lower.	

---

[33] A summary table of results can be found in Table D.5 in Appendix D.

Table 4.6
Summary of Results for RAND Base Area Social and Economic Index Domains: Results Associated with Higher Domain Scores, by Group

Domain	Measure	Active Duty	Reserve
Household composition	Likelihood to view military as a career	Higher	
	Base social cohesion (active duty) or neighborhood cohesion (reserve)	Lower[a]	Lower
	Satisfaction with Air Force way of life	Lower[b]	
	Satisfaction with community	Higher	
	Airman community engagement scale	Lower	Lower
	Perceived community safety	Higher	
	Perceived school quality	Higher	Higher
	Spending on child care	Higher	
	Self-rated health	Lower	
	Depressive symptoms	Higher	
Employment	Base social cohesion (active duty) or neighborhood cohesion (reserve)	Lower[a]	Lower
	Job resource subscale	Higher[a]	
	Perceived community safety	Higher[b]	
	Perceived school quality	Higher[b]	Higher
	Spending on child care	Higher	
	Depressive symptoms	Higher	
	Satisfaction with community		Higher
	Airman community engagement scale		Lower
	Perceived employer support		Lower[c]
Income and poverty	Base social cohesion	Lower[a]	
	Community satisfaction	Higher	Higher
	Airman community engagement scale	Lower	Lower
	Community resource scale	Higher[a, b]	
	Health care resource subscale	Higher[a]	
	Child-care resource subscale	Higher[a]	
	Job resource subscale	Higher[a, b]	
	Transportation resource subscale	Higher[a, b]	
	Child activity resource subscale	Higher[a, b]	
	Neighborhood cohesion	Lower[b]	
	Perceived school quality	Higher[b]	Higher

Domain	Measure	Active Duty	Reserve
	Spending on child care	Higher	Higher
	Economic stress scale	Lower	
	Perceived neighborhood support		Lower
	Perceived employer support		Lower[b]
Housing	Base social cohesion (active duty) or neighborhood cohesion (reserve)	Lower[a]	Higher
	Satisfaction with community	Higher	Higher
	Community resource scale	Higher[a, b]	
	Health care resource subscale	Higher[a, b]	
	Child-care resource subscale	Higher[a]	
	Job resource subscale	Higher[a]	
	Transportation resource subscale	Higher[a]	
	Child activity resource subscale	Higher[a, b]	
	Perceived community safety	Higher[b]	Higher
	Perceived child safety	Higher	
	Perceived school quality	Higher	Higher
	Exercise frequency	Lower	
	Airman community engagement scale		Lower
	Neighborhood support		Lower
Social	Base social cohesion (active duty) or neighborhood cohesion (reserve)	Lower[a, b]	Lower
	Satisfaction with base assignment	Higher[b]	Higher
	Satisfaction with Air Force way of life	Higher[b]	
	Satisfaction with community	Higher[b]	Higher
	Community resource scale	Higher[a, b]	
	Housing resource subscale	Higher[a, b]	
	Health care resource subscale	Higher[a, b]	
	Child-care resource subscale	Higher[a]	
	Job resource subscale	Higher[a, b]	
	Transportation resource subscale	Higher[a]	
	Child activity resource subscale	Higher[a, b]	
	Perceived community safety	Higher[b]	
	Perceived school quality	Higher[b]	Higher
	Spending on child care	Higher	Higher
	Economic stress scale	Lower	
	Financial stress		Lower[c]
Transportation	Satisfaction with base assignment	Lower	
	Satisfaction with Air Force way of life	Lower[b]	Higher

72

Domain	Measure	Active Duty	Reserve
	Community resource scale	Lower[a, b]	
	Housing resource subscale	Lower[a, b]	
	Health care resource scale	Lower[a, b]	
	Child-care resource scale	Lower[a, b]	
	Job resource subscale	Lower[a]	
	Transportation resource subscale	Lower[a]	
	Child activity subscale	Lower[a, b]	
	Neighborhood support	Higher[b]	Higher
	Spending on child care	Lower	Lower
	Economic stress	Higher	
	Depressive symptoms	Higher	
	Airman community engagement scale		Higher
	Neighborhood cohesion		Higher
	Perceived employer support		Higher[c]

[a] Asked only of active-duty Airmen.
[b] Supports the exposure hypothesis (i.e., the association between the domain and the outcome is stronger for Airmen who live off base than for those who live on base). This does not apply to the reserve.
[c] Asked only of reserve Airmen.

We can also draw a few other conclusions about our analysis of the Community Assessment Survey data. First, it does appear that our objective index of base-area quality is reflected by Airmen's subjective ratings. For example, among both active-duty and reserve Airmen, those who were assigned to and lived near base areas characterized by higher income, lower poverty rates, lower residential turnover, more affordable housing, more highly educated residents, more married families, and more military veterans (i.e., the overall RAND BASE-I, the income and poverty domain, the housing domain, and the social domain) were more satisfied with their communities.

Second, despite validation of the quality aspect of the scoring index and its domains, we did not find a lot of support for base-area characteristics having an impact on more-traditional health and well-being outcomes (e.g., self-rated health, depressive symptoms, exercise). There are several potential explanations for the lack of significant associations. In general, the sample is quite healthy. Most Airmen indicated that they exercised frequently, their health was good, and had few depressive symptoms. Second, for many outcomes, and not just those that can be considered traditional health measures (e.g., employer support, economic and financial stress), the variance around the mean is small. This means that most Airmen have outcomes that cluster very close to one another. The lower the variance, the less our multilevel models have to explain. Significant results are more difficult to detect when variance is low. Finally, we know that Airmen move frequently. Two to three years of exposure to any one base area may not be strong enough to have a discernible impact on health and well-being.

Third, and related to the idea of exposure to base-area characteristics, we found some evidence of an exposure effect via significant interactions.[34] Recall that we hypothesized that Airmen who lived off base would actually feel the effects of area characteristics more than Airmen who lived on base would. With no other measure of exposure to an area, residential status (i.e., on versus off base) was the best available proxy. When we did find evidence of a statistically significant interaction effect, it supported our hypothesis 81 percent of the time (48 out of 59 instances).

And fourth, when it is a significant predictor, the transportation domain is often associated with an outcome in the opposite direction from that predicted. That is, higher scores on the transportation domain are often associated with worse outcomes (e.g., lower satisfaction with base assignment or perception of fewer community resources). At first glance, this seems counterintuitive. Why would having a shorter commute time and greater access to automobiles within a community be associated with *worse* outcomes? As we noted above, higher scores on the transportation domain are found in more-rural areas. Although many Airmen and their families may enjoy living in more-rural areas, those areas may also provide them with fewer resources—everything from health care options to recreation and leisure activities (with some notable exceptions, such as hiking, hunting, or fishing). So it would appear that the transportation domain may really be a proxy for being located in a rural area.

---

[34] There were 168 opportunities for a significant interaction (i.e., the RAND BASE-I and six domains for each active-duty outcome). We found 59 statistically significant interactions (35 percent).

Chapter Five. Linking the RAND Base Area Social and Economic Index to Airman Outcomes: The 2010 Caring for People Survey

This chapter presents the results from a multilevel analysis of data from the 2010 Caring for People Survey. Separate models were run for active-duty and reserve Airmen. As with Chapter Four, we start by describing the sample, and then we describe outcomes regarding base programs and services, satisfaction with aspects of an Airman's neighborhood and military life in general, and service commitment. Along with those outcomes, we report the results of the multilevel analyses exploring whether these outcomes are associated with the RAND BASE-I.

Sample Description

This section describes the respondents included in our analyses according to base of assignment, residence relative to that base, and demographic characteristics, such as age, marital status, rank, and time at the current base. Retirees, spouses, and Air Force civilians who responded to the survey were not included in our analyses. Also, base areas for Creech, Fort George Meade, and the Pentagon were dropped from the analysis because no Airmen reported in the survey that they were assigned to those bases.

For most base areas, our 60-minute driving radius captured 90 percent or more of the survey respondents at each base in the Caring for People Survey. We calculated what percentage of both active-duty and reserve Airmen were included in that 60-minute radius, using resident ZIP Codes reported in the survey. Our analytic sample includes 94 percent of the roughly 38,000 military respondents from the Caring for People Survey. Coverage by base ranges from 80.8 percent (at MacDill AFB) to 100 percent (Arnold AFB).[35]

Active Duty

Of the roughly 33,500 Airmen in our analytic sample, 73 percent lived off base.[36] Those who lived off base were more educated and slightly older than their on-base peers.

---

[35] See Table E.1 in Appendix E.

[36] A detailed table of demographic statistics for active-duty Airmen in the analytic sample can be found in Table E.2 in Appendix E.

Most Airmen were married (68 percent), and just over half had at least one child (51 percent). Two-thirds of these children were secondary school age or younger: Twenty-eight percent were preschool age, and 39 percent were elementary or secondary school age.

The majority of Airmen in the analytic sample were enlisted rather than officers (77 percent versus 23 percent). In terms of rank, 24 percent of the overall sample were junior enlisted Airmen (E1–E4), 37 percent were junior noncommissioned officers (NCOs) (E5–E6), and 16 percent were senior NCOs (E7 and above). Approximately 11 percent of the sample were company-grade officers (O1–O3), 12 percent were field-grade officers (O4–O6), and less than 1 percent were general officers (O7 and above). In accordance with Air Force housing policy, junior enlisted Airmen were most likely to live on base.[37]

Years of service are associated with rank, and thus the demographic results are similar. Roughly 30 percent of Airmen in our analytic sample had served four or fewer years in the Air Force, meaning most if not all were in their first term of service commitment. About 21 percent of Airmen had served five to ten years, 36 percent were the "careerists" who had served ten to 20 years, and 14 percent had served 20 or more years.

More than 70 percent of Airmen in our analytic sample had been assigned to their current bases for more than one year. Fourteen percent had been at their current bases six months to 12 months, and 14 percent had spent less than six months there. Among the majority of Airmen who lived off base, roughly equal percentages rented versus owned. In addition to their basic pay, Airmen who live off base are given a basic allowance for housing (BAH) to help cover their housing expenses. The amount is based on their pay grade (rank), whether they have any dependents or not, and the housing costs where they are assigned. Airmen who live on base are not given a BAH because they are not charged for their housing. Airmen who live off base may choose to live in housing that is more or less expensive than their BAH. In our analytic sample, about 23 percent of Airmen who lived off base reported that their BAH covered 100 percent of their mortgage or rent. An additional 54 percent lived in housing that cost more than their BAH. The remainder (23 percent) reported that BAH covered more than their mortgage or rent, covering some of the cost of utilities as well.

---

[37] See Air Force Instruction 32-6005 (Secretary of the Air Force, 2011).

Reserve

We also prepared descriptive statistics for the reserve Airmen in our analytic sample.[38] We did not include Airmen assigned to smaller guard and reserve installations that did not meet our criteria for developing the RAND BASE-I (i.e., that had more than 1,000 permanent party personnel assigned). Our analyses include only reserve Airmen who were assigned to large, active-duty installations. Because reserve Airmen do not live on base, we present results for only the overall group.[39] Of our analytic sample of reserve Airmen, the majority were male (71 percent). Reserve Airmen were slightly older and more educated than their active-duty peers. Most (71 percent) were married, and roughly half (52 percent) had children. These children tended to be older than those of active-duty Airmen in our analytic sample, with 26 percent secondary school age and 24 percent elementary school age.

Airmen in the reserve are typically not employed full time by the Air Force.[40] Thus, it is important to know what an Airman's current employment status in the civilian sector is. Just over two-thirds of our sample were employed full time (69 percent) outside of their Air Force Reserve or Air National Guard commitments, and 5 percent were employed part time. Of the remaining population, 7 percent were unemployed but looking for work, 4 percent were unemployed but not looking for work, and 16 percent marked "other" on this survey question, which could mean they were students or were on leave or temporarily laid off from their civilian jobs.

Most of the reserve sample were enlisted Airmen (77 percent). Seven percent of the total sample reported being an E1 to E4, 34 percent were E5 to E6, 36 percent were E7 to E9, and 13 percent were E8 or above. The lowest-ranking officers, O1 to O3, were 5 percent of the sample; midlevel officers, O4 to O6, were 19 percent of the sample; and less than 1 percent were flag rank or above. Overall, most reserve Airmen in our sample had four or fewer years of experience, 31 percent had five to ten years of experience, 22 percent had ten to 20 years of experience, and only 2 percent had more than 20 years of experience.

Finally, although reserve Airmen do not live on base, they are assigned to a base for training and administrative purposes. They are free, however, to live anywhere they want relative to that base assignment. Roughly equally percentages of Airmen in our sample (40 percent) had been assigned to their current bases for less than six months and more

---

[38] A detailed table of demographic statistics for reserve Airmen in the analytic sample can be found in Table E.3 in Appendix E.

[39] BAH statistics are likewise not appropriate.

[40] Three percent of our reserve sample indicated that they were currently deployed.

than 12 months. Twenty-one percent had been assigned to their bases between six and 12 months.

Outcomes and Results from Multilevel Models

We explore a wide range of outcomes in the Caring for People Survey that could be linked to one's neighborhood (or base area), grouped into three categories: programs and services, satisfaction, and career. We first present the distribution of each outcome, by group, for four different groups of Airmen: all active-duty Airmen, active-duty Airmen who lived on base, active-duty Airmen who lived off base, and all reserve Airmen in our analytic sample. We then turn to the results from the multilevel models linking Airman outcomes to the RAND BASE-I and its domains, with each domain entered into the model separately (i.e., one domain per model).

In the sections that follow, we discuss only significant results from the full model (i.e., the model that includes control variables). For active-duty Airmen, the control variables include gender, age, education, marital status, age of children (if applicable), rank, years of service, time at current base, and BAH offset (if applicable). Control variables for reserve Airmen are the same except for BAH offset, which is not applicable. Employment status is included only as a control for reserve Airmen. All control variables occur at the individual level. That is, no base-level control variables (e.g., region, population density) are included. And, as we noted in Chapter Five, we have opted to present results based on statistical significance, versus a combination of statistical and practical significance. Nonetheless, interested readers can find effect sizes for the results presented in this chapter in Tables E.5 and E.6 in Appendix E. Again, these results represent *associations* between base-area conditions and individual Airman outcomes and should not be viewed as causal.

Programs and Services

The Caring for People Survey contained items about use of Air Force–provided programs and services. We wanted to assess whether Airmen who lived in base areas that score higher on the RAND BASE-I, which may have comparable resources, would be less likely to use programs or services provided by the Air Force. Table 5.1 shows the distribution of these outcomes across the four groups of Airmen.

Table 5.1

Program and Service Outcomes from the Caring for People Survey, by Group

Outcome	Total Active Duty	On Base	Off Base	Reserve
Total mean number of the 20 possible programs or services that the respondents endorsed	3.8 (1.3)	4.1 (1.2)	3.7 (1.4)	3.5 (1.4)
Use child and youth-related services (%)	41.4	42.1	41.1	36.4
Use recreation-related services (%)	59.9	67.0	57.3	48.8
Use food-related services (%)	79.9	82.7	78.8	85.7

NOTE: In parentheses are SDs.

Total Number of Services and Programs Used

The survey asked respondents to indicate whether or not they had used any of 20 different services or programs at their current bases in the past 12 months. These included the following:

- base dining facilities
- officers' or enlisted clubs
- other on-base food outlets (e.g., base exchange food court)
- libraries
- fitness centers
- intramural sports
- community centers
- outdoor recreation
- arts and crafts
- child development centers
- family child care
- Airman and Family Readiness Centers
- recovery care programs
- youth centers or programs
- tickets, tours, or travel
- golf courses or clubhouses
- bowling centers
- Aero Club
- sports clubs (e.g., Rod and Gun Club)
- auto hobbies or skills.

Airmen and their families who lived in base areas that score high on the RAND BASE-I, where community resources are more likely to be plentiful, may actually be more likely to use these types of services and programs off base, especially if they also lived off base, although, if these services are particularly expensive in the highest-scoring areas, on-base programs may still hold greater appeal. Conversely, if RAND BASE-I scores are low and community resources may not be available to Airmen or those spaces may not offer the safety or quality of on-base resources, they may be more likely to use services on base. We constructed a measure of the total number of services and programs that Airmen reported using in the previous year. In addition, we also created three dichotomous variables that indicate whether an Airman reported using any child- or youth-related service or program, recreation-related service or program, or food-related program.

As reported in Table 5.1, the average number of on-base services used by both active-duty and reserve Airmen in the previous year is about four. On-base Airmen used slightly more services and programs than those who lived off base (4.1 versus 3.7), although this difference is not substantively large. Roughly 40 percent had used a child or youth service or program.[41] More active-duty Airmen (60 percent) used recreation-related services and programs than reserve Airmen (49 percent) did. More than three-quarters of all Airmen reported using food-related services or programs in the previous year.

After reviewing the descriptive statistics for base program and service use, we used the multilevel modeling technique to explore whether usage is in any way associated with the RAND BASE-I (see Appendix E for details). We found that the overall RAND BASE-I does not have a significant association with the total number of on-base services and programs that active-duty Airmen and their families used. For reserve Airmen, however, living in a base area with a higher score on the RAND BASE-I is associated with using fewer on-base programs and services. It is possible that this association is simply picking up on the fact that reserve Airmen live off base and most of them also work off base. They may therefore have to make a more conscious choice or more of an effort to go on base to use on-base services and thus are more responsive to the characteristics of their off-base areas.

Two domains within the RAND BASE-I have a significant association with the number of services and programs Airmen and their families use.[42] More-desirable scores on the income and poverty domain (for both active duty and reserve) and the housing domain (reserve only) are associated with use of fewer on-base services and programs. That means that, where base-area income is higher and family poverty is lower, Airmen were less likely to use on-base resources, and the same is true for reservists where residents are spending a lower percentage of their income on housing and there are fewer

---

[41] Roughly 68 percent of parents reported using a child or youth service or program.

[42] Recall that these models contain only one domain. That is, each domain is included independently, without controlling for the other five constituent domains.

housing vacancies. More-desirable scores on the transportation domain, meaning shorter commutes to work and greater access to vehicles, are associated with greater use of on-base services and programs (for both active duty and reserve). Among active-duty Airmen, the associations found with the income and poverty and transportation domains are stronger for those who lived off base.

Use of Child- and Youth-Related Services

We restricted our multilevel model of use of youth-related programs and services to parents. The overall RAND BASE-I does not have a significant association with whether or not Airmen who were parents used child- and youth-related on-base programs or services. Higher scores on the household composition domain are positively associated with service and program use. Perhaps in areas where there are larger families (as measured by average household size) and more female-headed households, off-base child and youth services are stretched thin. If that is the case, then Air Force families may be more likely to use the services that only they are eligible to use because the community may be overtaxing civilian services.

Recreation-Related Services

Active-duty and reserve Airmen who lived in base areas that ranked higher on the overall RAND BASE-I were less likely to use on-base recreation-related activities than their peers who lived in lower-ranked base areas. It is possible that higher-scoring base areas have plenty of opportunities for leisure and recreation activities that are suitable alternatives to on-base activities. Higher scores on the income and poverty domain (both active duty and reserve) and the social domain (both active duty and reserve) are associated with lower odds of using on-base recreation services and programs. Higher scores on the transportation domain (both active duty and reserve) are associated with higher odds of using on-base recreation services and programs.

Food-Related Services

The overall RAND BASE-I does not have a significant association with whether or not Airmen used food-related on-base programs or services; however, higher scores on the income and poverty domain are associated with greater likelihood of using on-base food-related services and programs (both active duty and reserve). One possible explanation is that food options in these base areas are more expensive than those available to Airmen and their families on base; using on-base services and programs could be a way to save financial resources.

Summary of Service and Program Use

Overall, it appears that, in areas where commute times are low and people have access to their own transportation, barriers to using on-base services and programs may be lower. It also appears that Airmen who lived in areas defined by lower scores on the RAND BASE-I and specifically the income and social domain may have been more likely to use on-base services and programs. For these Airmen and their families, the Air Force may be providing options not available in the civilian community or may be offering more-desirable substitutes for existing options.

Life Satisfaction

The Caring for People Survey included a question about Airmen's satisfaction with life overall. Table 5.2 shows the distribution of this satisfaction outcome across the four groups of Airmen.

Table 5.2

Satisfaction Outcomes from the Caring for People Survey, by Group

Outcome	Total Active Duty	On Base	Off Base	Reserve
Life satisfaction, mean of three items	6.9 (2.2)	6.9 (2.2)	6.9 (2.1)	7.4 (2.0)

NOTE: The table shows mean values. The three items had possible ranges of 1 to 10 ("very dissatisfied" [1] to "very satisfied" [10], "fall short of my expectation" [1] to "exceeds my expectations" [10], or "not very close to ideal" [1] to "very close to ideal" [10]). Numbers in parentheses are SDs.

Three separate items asked about life satisfaction. The first asked Airmen how satisfied they were with their lives overall on a scale from "very dissatisfied" (1) to "very satisfied" (10). The second asked, "To what extent does your life today fall short of or exceed your expectations?" on a scale from "falls short of my expectations" (1) to "exceeds my expectations" (10). The third asked how close the Airman's life is today to the ideal, on a scale from "not very close to the ideal" (1) to "very close to the ideal" (10). Because these items shared the same numeric scale, we use an average score. We hypothesize that higher RAND BASE-I scores would be associated with higher life satisfaction scores. Across all Airmen, life satisfaction was approximately 7 on the ten-point scale (see Table 5.2).

Results from the multilevel models reveal that the RAND BASE-I does not have a significant association with Airman ratings of life satisfaction. For active-duty Airmen, the social domain is positively associated with life satisfaction, and the transportation domain is negatively associated with life satisfaction and is stronger for Airmen living off base. Interestingly, living in an area characterized by larger percentages of college-educated, married, and veteran residents is associated with higher ratings of life satisfaction. It is not clear why life satisfaction and the transportation domain are inversely related. One would assume that shorter commute times would be associated with higher life satisfaction (as they are with financial satisfaction); however, the transportation domain does not contain any information on where those base areas are that facilitate shorter commute times. So, if those areas are low quality in other measures, extremely rural, or very close to industrial areas, it may be that a short commute time is actually a negative rather than a positive.[43]

Neighborhood Resources

The Caring for People Survey also included questions about Airmen's satisfaction with various aspects of their neighborhood resources, including their neighborhoods, quality of current housing, health care, number of civilian friends, leisure, finances, and life overall. Table 5.3 shows the distribution of these satisfaction outcomes across the four groups of Airmen.

---

[43] Recall that we did not include a measure of rurality in the RAND BASE-I because it is not clear whether more or less rural is "better" in some objective sense. Ultimately, the merits of living in a rural versus urban area are a matter of personal choice or preference.

Table 5.3
Neighborhood Resource Outcomes from the Caring for People Survey, by Group

Outcome	Total Active Duty	On Base	Off Base	Reserve
Neighborhood rating scale[a]	7.6 (1.7)	7.7 (1.7)	7.6 (1.7)	7.9 (1.5)
Satisfaction with quality of housing[b]	7.8 (1.8)	7.1 (2.1)	8.0 (1.6)	8.3 (1.5)
Satisfaction with health care[c]	7.5 (2.2)	7.5 (2.3)	7.5 (2.2)	8.0 (2.0)
Satisfaction with number of civilian friends[d]	6.8 (2.7)	6.7 (2.9)	6.9 (2.7)	7.8 (2.3)
Leisure[e]	6.7 (2.0)	6.7 (2.1)	6.8 (2.0)	7.2 (1.9)
Financial[f]	6.5 (2.3)	6.4 (2.4)	6.5 (2.3)	6.7 (2.3)

[a] Mean of ten items, possible range "poor" (1) to "excellent" (10).
[b] Mean of eight items, possible range "poor" (1) to "excellent" (10).
[c] Mean of two items, possible range "poor" (1) to "excellent" (10).
[d] Possible range "very dissatisfied" (1) to "very satisfied" (10).
[e] Mean of five items, possible range "poor" (1) to "excellent" (10).
[f] Mean of four items, possible range "very dissatisfied" (1) to "very satisfied" (10).
NOTE: The table shows mean values. Numbers in parentheses are SDs.

Neighborhood Rating Scale

We created a ten-item, subjective neighborhood rating scale. It provides an opportunity to corroborate the RAND BASE-I, which is an objective measure of neighborhood quality. Airmen were asked to rate their current neighborhoods on eight characteristics on a scale from "poor" (1) to "excellent" (10):

- safety
- public services (e.g., trash, mail, police)
- general appearance
- transportation services
- sense of community
- retail services (e.g., grocery, dry cleaning)
- availability or parking
- commute time to work.

In general, Airmen rated their neighborhoods quite highly, with an average score of 8 regardless of component or on- or off-base status (see Table 5.3).

Results from the multilevel models show that, among active-duty Airmen, living in a higher-rated RAND BASE-I area is associated with higher subjective ratings of one's neighborhood. However, we found that this was true only among active-duty Airmen who lived off base. A similar pattern emerged for the income and poverty, housing, and social domains (active duty only).

These findings serve as a good check that our objective index is measuring some aspect of base-area quality. However, we found a negative association between the transportation domain and subjective neighborhood ratings (active duty only), and this association was limited to Airmen who lived off base. It is not entirely clear why shorter commute times and greater access to automobiles would be associated with lower subjective ratings of neighborhood quality. Perhaps those specific areas that allow for shorter commute times are less desirable places to live. We also found evidence of an exposure effect in the income and poverty, housing, social, and transportation domains. That is, the association between the domain and Airmen's qualitative rating of their neighborhoods was stronger for those who lived off base than for those who lived on base.

Satisfaction with Quality of Current Housing

Eight survey items asked Airmen to rate their satisfaction with their current housing. Airmen may be more likely to express higher satisfaction with their housing if they live in high-quality base areas as indicated by higher scores on the RAND BASE-I. We use the mean of the following eight items, rated from "poor" (1) to "excellent" (10):

- attractiveness of your housing
- amenities in your housing (e.g., appliances)
- privacy of housing
- size of housing
- location of housing
- comfort of housing
- condition of housing
- affordability of housing.

In general, Airmen were satisfied with their current housing, although those who lived off base (8.0) and reserve Airmen (8.3) reported slightly higher levels of satisfaction than their on-base peers (7.1; see Table 5.3).

According to the multilevel models, reserve Airmen who lived in areas with higher scores on the RAND BASE-I actually reported lower levels of satisfaction with their current housing. This is not true for active-duty Airmen. Similar results occur for the household composition domain (active duty and reserve), employment domain (active duty and reserve), and the transportation domain (active duty and reserve). With the exception of the income and poverty domain, when the interaction term is significant, the associations are stronger for Airmen who lived off base. So, in base areas with few female-headed households, low unemployment rates, low (family) poverty rate, and short commute times, Airmen were less satisfied than those who lived in base areas with less desirable characteristics.

Overall, these results suggest that Airmen were not entirely satisfied with the characteristics of their current housing when they were assigned to higher-scoring base areas. What our results cannot differentiate is why this is the case. It could be due to a lack of satisfactory housing in the civilian area around certain AFBs, Airmen not being able to afford satisfactory housing, or Airmen purposely selecting housing that is not satisfactory (e.g., to save money). It could also be that reserve Airmen had higher expectations for their housing in areas that score well on the RAND BASE-I simply because they were more aware of the quality of housing in the surrounding area. Thus, a high-scoring base area may actually negatively influence subjective ratings of certain aspects of life, such as satisfaction with housing, because of a social comparison effect.

Satisfaction with Health Care

Two survey items captured Airmen's satisfaction with access to medical care for themselves and their families and the quality of care they receive. We take the mean of these two items, which ranges from "poor" (1) to "excellent" (10). Although most Airmen have access to military health care, some opt to use out-of-network care or may have special needs that require utilization of nonmilitary providers (e.g., rare diseases, unique or nontraditional treatments). Thus, it is possible that higher scores on the RAND BASE-I are associated with higher satisfaction with health care. Overall, Airmen were highly satisfied with both access and receipt of care, with reserve Airmen's ratings slightly higher than those of their active-duty peers (8.0 versus 6.5; see Table 5.3).

The multilevel analysis shows that active-duty Airmen who lived in base areas that score higher on the overall RAND BASE-I reported greater satisfaction with health care. This is not true for reserve Airmen. A positive association appears for the income and poverty domain (active duty only), the housing domain (active duty only), and the social domain (active duty only). For the social domain, the association is positive only for Airmen who lived off base. So Airmen who lived in base areas where unemployment rates are low, residential turnover is low, affordable housing is plentiful, and larger percentages of the population are married, hold a college degree, and are military veterans were more satisfied with both quality of and access to health care for themselves and their families. The association between the transportation domain and satisfaction with health care is negative (active duty only) and stronger for Airmen who lived off base. So, for Airmen who lived in base areas characterized by lower commute times and greater access to automobiles, satisfaction with health care was lower. Taken together, these results suggest that availability and quality of health care were higher in areas that score higher on the RAND BASE-I.

Satisfaction with Number of Civilian Friends

One item assesses Airmen satisfaction with the number of civilian friends they had on a scale from "very dissatisfied" (1) to "very satisfied" (10). Satisfaction with civilian friends may be a proxy for community integration, social cohesion, and social capital. We hypothesized that Airmen assigned to base areas that score higher on the RAND BASE-I would have higher satisfaction with the number of civilian friends they have. Active-duty Airmen reported slightly lower satisfaction levels (6.8) than their reserve peers (7.8; see Table 5.3).

According to the multilevel models, the RAND BASE-I is not significantly associated with Airmen's satisfaction with the number of civilian friends that they have. However, the social domain is positively associated with satisfaction ratings (active duty and reserve), and the association is significant only among active-duty Airmen who live off base. Recall that one of the indicators in the social domain is the percentage of the area's population who are military veterans. Thus, it could be that current Airmen are more satisfied with their civilian friendships when more veterans are located in the community. Also, the social domain was intended to capture, albeit indirectly, some positive elements of social capital and social cohesion. The positive association between the domain and this outcome suggests that the domain does indeed measure some aspect of those constructs. The transportation domain is negatively associated with satisfaction with the number of civilian friends (both active duty and reserve), and this association is stronger for Airmen who live off base. Again, it may be that those base areas that allow for shorter commute times are not as high quality and are low in social capital and social cohesion.

Leisure Satisfaction

Airman satisfaction with leisure activities, both on and off base, is measured by taking the mean of five items:

- the variety of leisure activities available
- the affordability of leisure activities available
- the facilities available for leisure activities
- the amount of leisure time one has
- ease of finding information about leisure activities.

Each item is rated on a scale from "poor" (1) to "excellent" (10). Rating on leisure should be positively correlated with the scores on the RAND BASE-I. Average satisfaction with leisure is roughly 7 on the scale, with ratings slightly higher among reserve Airmen than among active duty (7.2 versus 6.7; see Table 5.3).

Results from the multilevel models show that the overall RAND BASE-I is not significantly associated with Airman satisfaction ratings of leisure time and activities. We did find a positive association between the income and poverty domain (active duty only), the social domain (active duty only), and leisure satisfaction. These associations were stronger among Airmen who lived off base. We found a negative association between the transportation domain (active duty only) and leisure satisfaction, and this association was stronger for Airmen who lived off base. The results suggest one of two possibilities. First, high-scoring base areas (i.e., those with higher SES as measured by income, poverty, and education) have more, and higher-quality, leisure activities. Second, individuals who live in higher-quality areas have more resources to participate in satisfying leisure activities. Unfortunately, our analysis is not causal, so we cannot tease apart these two explanations.

Financial Satisfaction

Financial satisfaction is measured by the average satisfaction level reported on four survey items:

- the money one has available for essentials
- the money one has available for extras
- one's ability to save money for general needs
- one's ability to save for retirement.

Items are rated on a scale from "very dissatisfied" (1) to "very satisfied" (10). Although base areas with higher scores on the RAND BASE-I may be of higher quality, they may also be very expensive. Thus, we might expect a negative association between financial satisfaction and RAND BASE-I scores. Conversely, because Airmen are generally well compensated, this association may be positive, with Airmen reporting higher financial satisfaction in higher-rated base areas. Satisfaction ratings ranged from 6.5 among on-base, active-duty Airmen to 6.7 among reserve Airmen (see Table 5.3).

According to the multilevel models, the RAND BASE-I does not have a significant association with Airman ratings of financial satisfaction. In fact, only one domain—transportation—has a significant association with this outcome, once controls are included in the model. Reserve Airmen who lived in base areas with lower commute times and greater access to an automobile reported greater financial satisfaction. It is possible that having a shorter commute time may save money (e.g., in gas and wear and tear on automobiles) and time, leading to higher satisfaction with one's financial situation.

Career

Three different survey items addressed Airmen's military service and military career intentions. The first asked how likely it is that the Airman would either reenlist when his or her current obligation is completed (if enlisted) or serve past his or her present service commitment (if officer). The second asked whether the Airman is likely to stay in the Air

Force until retirement. This question was asked only of Airmen with eight or fewer years of service. The third item, asked only of reserve Airmen, asked how the respondent's service in the Air Force Reserve or Air National Guard has affected his or her civilian career. Table 5.4 shows the distribution of the career outcomes across the four groups of Airmen.

Table 5.4
Satisfaction Outcomes from the Caring for People Survey, by Group

Outcome	Total Active Duty	On Base	Off Base	Reserve
Remain past obligation or reenlist[a]	6.5 (3.4)	6.7 (3.3)	6.5 (3.4)	7.5 (3.1)
Career intention[a]	6.0 (3.3)	6.1 (3.4)	6.0 (3.3)	8.6 (2.4)
Impact of military career on civilian work[b]	N/A	N/A	N/A	3.4 (1.2)

[a] Possible range "not at all likely" (1) to "very likely" (10).
[b] Question asked only of the reserve. Possible range "very negatively" (1) to "very positively" (5).
NOTE: The table shows mean values. Numbers in parentheses are SDs.

Remain Past Obligation or Reenlist

We hypothesized that higher scores on the RAND BASE-I would be associated with greater likelihood of service continuation and career intentions, if exposure during a tour of duty is long enough to have an impact. Similarly, we hypothesized that reserve Airmen who lived in higher-quality base areas, as rated by the RAND BASE-I, would be more likely to consider remaining in the Air Force long term. Service continuation ranges from 6.5 among active-duty Airmen who lived off base to 7.5 among reserve Airmen (see Table 5.4).

According to the multilevel model results, reserve Airmen who lived in more-favorable base areas (i.e., have higher scores on the overall RAND BASE-I) reported a lower self-rated likelihood of remaining in the Air Force past a current obligation or reenlisting. The employment domain and the housing domain also show negative associations with continuation and reenlistment among only the reserve. These results suggest that Airmen may forgo the Air Force for other opportunities in the civilian sector in base areas where the economy is doing well. For active-duty Airmen, higher scores on the household composition domain and the transportation domain are negatively associated with continuation and reenlistment. The social domain is positively associated with continuation and reenlistment.

Career Intentions

Career intentions were higher among reserve Airmen than among active duty (8.6 versus 6.0; see Table 5.4). Career intentions are also negatively associated with the overall RAND BASE-I among reserve Airmen; that is, reserve Airmen in more-favorable base areas were less likely to report wanting to stay in the Air Force until they are eligible for full retirement benefits. The same is true for the employment and income and poverty domains. Again, this suggests that, when reserve Airmen have other opportunities, they are less likely to see the Air Force as a career. For active-duty Airmen, the RAND BASE-I is not a predictor of career intentions. However, the household composition and transportation domains have a negative association with career intentions, and the income and poverty and social domains have a positive association with career intentions. So, in contrast to their reserve peers, when base areas are doing well economically, active-duty Airmen were actually *more* likely to say they view the Air Force as a career. Two caveats are worth mentioning. First, the association is significant only for Airmen who live off base. Perhaps Airmen who live on base are simply not aware of civilian opportunities. Second, career *intentions* are not deterministic: That is, the fact an Airman says that he or she intends to remain in the Air Force until retirement does not mean that his or her behavior will actually reflect this intention. However, some research suggests that "turnover intentions [are] the strongest, most direct precursor of turnover behavior, and [mediate] the relationship between attitudes like job satisfaction and organizational commitment and turnover behavior" (Jaros, 1997, p. 321; see also Guthrie, 1992; Marsh, 1989; Janega and Olmsted, 2003; Jans and Frazer-Jans, 2006). We should also point out that retention *intentions* can be viewed as one of the proximate outcomes referenced in Figure 1.1 in Chapter One, which can help the Air Force understand actual retention *behavior*, a more distal outcome.

Impact of Military Career on Work

Overall, reserve Airmen reported that their service has had no real effect on their civilian careers, with a mean roughly equivalent to 3 on the five-point scale (see Table 5.4). We found no significant associations between the RAND BASE-I or the six domains and reserve Airmen's ratings of how their military careers had affected their civilian work. Given that the average rating on the outcome was "no impact," we are not surprised by this result.

Discussion

In this chapter, we presented results from multilevel models linking the RAND BASE-I and its six constituent domains to various measures of the well-being of Airmen and their families.[44] Overall, we find some evidence that base-area quality, as measured by the RAND BASE-I, does matter for different aspects of well-being, service utilization, and retention intentions (see Figure 5.1 and Table 5.5). However, we cannot definitely determine whether these associations are causal—that is, whether living in a specific type of area is the reason that some Airmen have better (or worse) outcomes than others. It is also possible that Airmen with certain characteristic (e.g., higher SES) self-select into higher-quality base areas, which would make any association between the RAND BASE-I and its domains and Airman outcomes spurious. Nonetheless, the relationship between the RAND BASE-I and Airman outcomes would still hold; however, as noted above, we would not be able to make causal claims about these relationships.

Figure 5.1
Summary of Results for Overall RAND Base Area Social and Economic Index for the Caring for People Survey, by Group

Base areas with higher RAND BASE-I scores	
Active Duty	**Reserve**
√ Are less likely to use on-base recreation-related services.	√ Use fewer on-base programs and services.
√ Rate subjective neighborhood quality higher.	√ Are less likely to use on-base recreation-related services.
√ Report greater satisfaction with access to and quality of health care for self and family.	√ Report lower satisfaction with quality of current housing.
	√ Report lower self-rated likelihood of continuation or reenlistment.
	√ Are less likely to report intention of staying in Air Force until retirement.

Table 5.5
Summary of Results for RAND Base Area Social and Economic Index Domains: Results Associated with Higher Domain Scores, by Group

Domain	Measure	Active Duty	Reserve
Household composition	Likelihood to use child and youth services	Higher	
	Satisfaction with housing	Lower[a]	Lower
	Financial satisfaction	Lower	
	Likelihood to remain past obligation or reenlist	Lower	

---

[44] A summary table of results can be found in Table E.4 in Appendix E.

91

Domain	Measure	Active Duty	Reserve
	Likelihood to view military as a career	Lower	
Employment	Satisfaction with quality of housing		Lower
	Likelihood to remain past obligation or reenlist		Lower
	Likelihood to view military as a career		Lower
Income and poverty	Number of base programs and services used	Lower[a]	Lower
	Likelihood to use food services	Higher	Higher
	Likelihood to use recreation services	Lower	Lower
	Neighborhood rating scale	Higher[a]	
	Satisfaction with health care	Higher	
	Satisfaction with leisure	Higher[a]	
	Likelihood to view military as a career	Higher[a]	Lower
	Likelihood to use child and youth services		Higher
	Satisfaction with housing		Lower
Housing	Neighborhood rating scale	Higher[a]	
	Satisfaction with health care	Higher	
	Number of base programs and services used		Lower
	Likelihood to remain past obligation or reenlist		Lower
Social	Likelihood to use recreation services	Lower	Lower
	Neighborhood rating scale	Higher[a]	
	Satisfaction with health care	Higher[a]	
	Satisfaction with number of civilian friends	Higher[a]	Higher
	Leisure satisfaction	Higher[a]	
	Life satisfaction	Higher[a]	
	Likelihood to remain past obligation or reenlist	Higher[a]	
	Likelihood to view military as a career intention	Higher[a]	
Transportation	Number of base programs and services used	Higher[a]	Higher
	Likelihood to use recreation services	Higher	Higher
	Neighborhood rating scale	Lower[a]	
	Satisfaction with housing	Lower[a]	Lower
	Satisfaction with health care	Lower[a]	
	Satisfaction with number of civilian friends	Lower[a]	
	Leisure satisfaction	Lower[a]	
	Life satisfaction	Lower[a]	
	Likelihood to remain past obligation or reenlist	Lower[a]	
	Likelihood to view military as a career	Lower[a]	
	Financial satisfaction		Higher

[a] Supports the exposure hypothesis (i.e., the association between the domain and the outcome is stronger for Airmen who live off base than for those who live on base). Does not apply to reserve component.

We can also draw some other conclusions based on this analysis. First, we found some evidence that our index does match subjective quality of neighborhood. Airmen who were assigned to and lived near base areas that we objectively defined as high quality, as indicated by high scores on the RAND BASE-I, the income and poverty domain (i.e., higher income and lower poverty rates), the housing domain (i.e., residential turnover is low, and affordable housing is plentiful), and the social domain (i.e., larger percentages of the population are married, hold a college degree, and are military veterans), rated the quality of their neighborhoods higher than those who lived in base areas where the RAND BASE-I is lower.

Second, when we tested for an interaction between the RAND BASE-I and its domains and whether an Airman lived on base, we did find some stronger associations for Airmen who lived off base, in the civilian community. In terms of exposure to base-area characteristics, we hypothesized that area might matter more if an Airman worked on base but lived elsewhere. However, given that not all interactions were significant and not all that were significant favored off-base Airmen, at best, our results provide modest support for this hypothesis.

And third, we found more-significant associations between the RAND BASE-I and its domains (especially income and poverty, social, and transportation) for active-duty versus reserve Airmen. Many of the survey items in the Caring for People Survey may be more relevant for active-duty Airmen, especially those who live on base. We also know that we do not capture as many reserve Airmen in our 60-mile-radius definition of base areas as we do active-duty Airmen. These two factors may have limited our ability to detect significant associations among the reserve.

Chapter Six. Summary, Conclusion, and Policy Recommendations

The goal of this study was to provide the Air force with additional data with which it could more effectively and efficiently distribute resources at the base level and target its programming to ensure that those with the greater need have the appropriate type of Air Force resources available to them. To do this, we first developed the RAND BASE-I using social and economic indicators from census data. The results of this analysis showed that there is a great deal of variation in the quality and characteristics of the areas around Air Force installations where Airmen and their families live. Especially prominent are the economic disparities across some of these communities. The objective was not to place negative or positive attention on any particular bases but to provide a greater understanding of the context in which military personnel and their families live. The better Air Force headquarters can understand the lives of Air Force personnel and their families, the better it can help counteract the negative influences and provide or harness existing community resources.

After developing the RAND BASE-I, we explored whether there was an association between these base-area scores and outcomes at the individual Airman level. Table 6.1 provides a high-level summary of the results.[45] We found few associations between more-traditional health and well-being measures (e.g., self-rated health, depressive symptoms) and scores on the RAND BASE-I. One possible reason for this is the fact that Airmen are, on the whole, a healthy group. Service members also move frequently, which means the characteristics of their environments may also change. Frequent relocation may limit the impact any given base area may have on individual-level outcomes. This is an area in which the civilian literature has little to say because residential stability is generally much higher.

We did find that the RAND BASE-I is significantly associated with Airmen's ratings of the level of military and neighborhood social cohesion they perceived, with higher-quality base areas generally associated with lower levels of cohesion, especially on the base. Airmen who lived in higher-quality base areas were generally more satisfied with resources available to them. The overall RAND BASE-I is positively associated with

---

[45] Note that these results are based primarily on tests of statistical significance. Readers interested in the strength, or magnitudes, of these significant associations are referred to tables that present effect sizes in Appendixes D and E.

Airmen's subjective ratings of their neighborhoods, providing evidence that our objective measure is correlated with subjective beliefs. Perhaps not surprisingly, Airmen who lived in higher-quality base areas also reported using fewer on-base resources, especially outdoor recreation-related resources. And, in terms of career outcomes, we found that the RAND BASE-I is a significant predictor only among reserve Airmen, who perceived less support from employers and were less likely to report career military intentions if they lived in a higher-quality base areas.

Table 6.1
Summary of Results: The Association Between Airman Outcomes and the RAND Base Area Social and Economic Index

Outcome	Significant Association with RAND BASE-I
Health and well-being	No
Military and neighborhood social cohesion	Yes
Ratings of neighborhood resources	Yes
Use of on-base resources	Yes
Satisfaction	Yes
Career	Only for reserve

Finally, we found some support for the exposure hypothesis. The exposure hypothesis suggests that the impact of neighborhood characteristics may be stronger for individuals who are more "exposed" to their neighborhoods. In the context of the military, we operationalized exposure as living either on (i.e., less exposed) or off (i.e., more exposed) base. Of course, there are other ways to quantify exposure (e.g., hours spent in one's neighborhood). Data limitations prevented us from using such measures.

Highlights from RAND Base Area Social and Economic Index Results

Although Table 6.1 provides an overview of our findings, we also provide a summary of more-specific results based on the six broad outcome categories we examined. At higher-scoring base areas, as measured by the RAND BASE-I, active-duty Airmen reported

- lower levels of base social cohesion
- lower levels of Airman engagement in the base community
- greater perceived community safety
- higher satisfaction with community resources
- higher satisfaction with the local base area

- higher satisfaction with access to and the quality of health care
- lower economic stress
- higher school quality
- spending more on child care
- being less likely to use on-base recreational services
- higher neighborhood quality ratings.

We found both some similarities and some differences in the results for reserve Airmen. At higher-scoring base areas, reservists reported

- lower Airman engagement in the base community
- lower neighborhood social cohesion
- higher school quality
- using fewer on-base programs and services
- being less likely to use on-base recreational services
- higher satisfaction with base assignment
- higher satisfaction with the local base area
- lower satisfaction with quality of one's own housing
- less support from employers
- lower likelihood of continuation or reenlistment
- lower likelihood staying in the Air Force until retirement.

Here there may be a need for some additional research to understand why reservists in higher-scoring base areas were less satisfied with their housing, perceived less support from their employers, and showed lower levels of commitment to the Air Force.

Other Types of Social Indicators the Air Force Could Consider

We used census data as the source of the social indicators data used to construct the RAND BASE-I. We did so for several reasons, including consistency across geographic units, objectivity, cost, ease of use, and use in other social indicators research. This is not to say, however, that an index of social and economic characteristics of a neighborhood or geographic area must use census data.

When developing the RAND BASE-I, we considered other measures of neighborhood and area quality. Although we did not include them, they should be noted in the event that others in the Air Force or U.S. Department of Defense (DoD) would like to use a similar methodology. We focus on three indicators in our discussion, but readers should not infer that these are the only three other types of information about neighborhoods or areas that could be included in a social indicators index: school quality, safety, and environmental hazards.[46]

School Quality

In our analysis of the Community Assessment Survey data, we found that higher scores on the overall RAND BASE-I, as well as five of the six domains (the exception being the transportation domain), were associated with higher levels of perceived school quality. Although we used perceived school quality as an outcome, it is also possible to use school quality as an indicator of neighborhood or area quality. The census data we used to construct the RAND BASE-I (the ACS) do not contain a direct measure of school quality. However, there is some evidence that school quality and, ultimately, student performance are positively correlated with neighborhood SES, which we do capture in the RAND BASE-I (Dupere et al., 2010; Johnson, 2011). Thus, we likely have an indirect measure of school quality. Other, more-direct measures of school quality may include such things as student-to-teacher ratio, expenditures per student, student performance (e.g., standardized test scores, teacher performance; for other examples, see Schwartz et al., 2011). School quality measures that can be compared across units of geography are preferred to those that may vary by location.

Safety

Another indicator of neighborhood quality would be direct measures of safety. In our analysis of the Community Assessment data, we found that Airmen who lived in higher-scoring base areas, as assessed by the overall RAND BASE-I, perceived their neighborhoods to be safer than did Airmen who lived in lower-scoring base areas. They also rated the safety of their children on their way to and from school as higher. Given existing literature that suggests that neighborhood crime (and fear of crime) is associated with low-quality areas (e.g., low SES, high social disorganization or disorder), this finding is not surprising (Bursik and Grasmick, 1993; Sampson, 1985; Scarborough et al., 2010). As with school quality, direct measures of crime could be used in a neighborhood, or area, quality index. Such measures might include arrest rates, victimization rates, or insurance claim rates. These data are generally standardized across the country but may not be available at a unit of analysis (e.g., ZIP Code versus state level) that is useful (see Hipp, 2007) or consistent with other types of data.

---

[46] Other quality indicators include retail or zoning mix, including the food environment, neighborhood disorder or disorganization, and walkability.

Environmental Hazards

A third type of neighborhood quality indicator that could be considered is related to environmental hazards. This could range from the presence of poisonous or noxious chemical in water or soil to the walkability of a neighborhood. It could even include climate, average temperatures, or annual rainfall, although what the preferred type of weather would be for different outcomes (e.g., neighborhood cohesion, health and well-being) would need to be established, which makes it difficult to rank-order geographies. Long-term exposure to neighborhood environmental hazards may result in increased stress levels. Obviously, short-term exposure to pollution and toxic waste can have immediate, negative effects on health. Prolonged exposure to stress associated with exposure to neighborhood environmental hazards may result in "weathering" of the body's ability to physically and mentally cope with negative stimuli (Ellen, Mijanovich, and Dillman, 2001). Because many environmental stressors are associated with low-income areas, individuals who live in such areas may be disproportionately affected by certain types of environmental hazards (e.g., lead paint, pollution, rodents and insect infestation, crumbling sidewalks). Again, should these types of indicators of neighborhood quality be included in a social index, they should be comparable across geographic units.

Ultimately, one must consider whether the resources necessary to find or collect other measures of neighborhood quality offer explanatory power beyond existing and readily available measures of neighborhood SES. If so, they may be worth the investment. If not, it may be more practical to use existing data, which may serve as sufficient proxies anyway.

Limitations of Social Indicators Research and Neighborhood and Area Research

Although we addressed the limitations of neighborhood research in Chapter One, many are worth repeating because they help contextualize our results. First and foremost, correlation does not equal causation. That is, the fact that neighborhood, or area, quality and characteristics are associated with individual-level outcomes does not mean that those characteristics *caused* the observed outcome. Individuals have the ability to select where they live, even most individuals in the military (although one could argue that they face more constraints than do their civilian counterparts). As a result, healthier and wealthier individuals may choose to live in higher-quality neighborhoods.

Second, there is not an accepted universal way in which to measure *neighborhood*. Two people who live next door to each other may have very different conceptualizations of what their neighborhoods are. This limitation may result in an underestimation of the association between neighborhood or area characteristics and individual outcomes. And, as noted above, because service members and their families are a highly mobile population, definitions of *neighborhood* or *area* may be fluid, changing over time. We also noted in Chapter Two that the size of our base areas are generally much larger than the neighborhoods used in existing civilian literature, although some studies consider the characteristics of large areas, such as counties or states.

Third, even if a researcher is able to define *neighborhood* in a meaningful way, neighborhoods and areas differ on a variety of dimensions (e.g., characteristics of the people who live there, characteristics of the physical environment, characteristics of the businesses and industries located there). Should one measure these characteristics in the aggregate, or as specific, individual qualities? Is neighborhood SES best measured by poverty rates, or by poverty, employment, and income combined? And is SES alone enough to accurately describe a neighborhood and its impact on individual outcomes? Ultimately, the answers to these questions require a theoretical base and empirical evidence. We utilized a well-known method to synthesize neighborhood quality across neighborhood characteristics, yet there are other ways to construct such an index, as we note in Appendix B.

Social indicators research also has limitations, many of which apply to this study. First, any aggregate index is only as accurate as the data from which it is composed. We feel confident in the accuracy of the census data used here. However, we could also have used other, attitudinal self-reported survey data to construct a base-area quality index, or paid to use proprietary data. We are not saying that these types of data are inaccurate. Rather, we are arguing that these other types of data may reflect *perceptions* of neighborhood characteristics, such as crime or unemployment rates that differ from those actual statistics.

Second, some indicators may be more influential than others in affecting health and well-being. We opted to weight each of the six domains in the RAND BASE-I equally, which means that not all 20 indicators are weighted equally.[47] Without a priori reasons for *unequal* weighting of indicators or domains, this is the preferred methodology (Hagerty and Land, 2007). But, given the flexibility of social indicators indices, changing the weighting to reflect differential importance of indicators and domains is relatively easy. We caution, however, that, without a strong theoretical or policy-relevant reason to unequally weight an index, the results should be interpreted with caution.

---

[47] We did calculate an equally weighted *indicator* RAND BASE-I (the RAND BASE-I[I]), on which all 20 indicators are given equal weights (see Table B.2 in Appendix B). Results from the RAND BASE-I(I) closely resemble those of the RAND BASE-I.

Third, and related to the prior limitation, the mix of indicators we used in the construction of the RAND BASE-I is open to debate. We provided theoretical reasons for having selected the indicators we used—in some ways, we see them as reflective of different elements of base-area quality. We also presented some omitted indicators (e.g., racial composition, region, population density) that are related to the RAND BASE-I but that we did not include because the labels of "good" versus "bad" were far less clear than for those indicators that we did include. Future work should address the issue of omitted indicators, as well as further validations of the index methodology in general. Although we believe that a composite view of base-area quality is valuable, it is also possible that, in isolation, some subset of indicators (or even a single indicator) may convey just as much information. Such research would address whether the index can be distilled into some optimal combination of indicators. It is also possible that a restricted group of indicators may have a more powerful association with certain outcomes than others (e.g., family poverty rates may be more predictive of child outcomes than access to automobiles).

Fourth, and perhaps most important, an index does not inherently have anything to say about "best" or "worst." Even the base area that scores the highest on the RAND BASE-I could, in theory, be improved (i.e., have even lower family poverty rates, have even more employed citizens, have even lower residential turnover). A social index is simply a way to compare and rank entities, whether they are states, years, or AFB areas. As such, the RAND BASE-I is intended to be another piece of information the Air Force can use to make decisions about resource allocation. It should not stand alone.

Practical Application of Neighborhood and Area Social Indicators for Air Force Leaders

We offer examples for the practical application of neighborhood and area social indicators for Air Force leaders. We focus on three groups across the Air Force: Air Force Services, Air Force Medical Service, and installation commanders. In this section, we offer practical advice for how each group could use the methodology we used in this study to help them think about support for Airmen and their families. We conclude with a discussion of how other researchers interested in military populations may also use neighborhood and area social indicators to enhance their own work.

How Air Force Services Can Use Neighborhood and Area Quality Data

The primary objective of the current study was to help the Air Force more efficiently and effectively tailor and distribute base-level resources. We argue that the RAND BASE-I and indices like it provide one set of tools the Air Force can use to make policy decisions about the allocation of limited or scarce resources. Although this is a general recommendation, we offer five specific examples of how the results from this study can be used by Air Force Services.

First, increase or develop programs to foster a sense of community at higher-scoring bases. Airmen who live near base areas that ranked higher on the RAND BASE-I reported lower levels of base cohesion. Ideally, programs to address this issue would leverage local base leadership, as well as local community leadership, to promote greater interaction and the Wingman Culture.

Second, focus spouse employment assistance resources to areas with high unemployment. A large literature examines the impact of being a service member's spouse on employment opportunities (Cooke and Speirs, 2005; Harrell et al., 2004; Hosek et al., 2002; Lim, Golinelli, and Cho, 2007). A recent report by Lim and Schulker (2010) finds that military wives are more likely to be underemployed than members of a group of similar (or "look-alike") civilian wives.[48] Military wives are also more likely to not be in the labor force, work fewer hours than they would like, and be overqualified for their jobs (i.e., have more education than necessary for their position). With the existing literature and our finding that Airmen who live near base areas that score high on the overall RAND BASE-I and the employment and income and poverty domains are more satisfied with community job resources, Air Force Services may consider "beefing up" employment services for Airmen transitioning out of the Air Force, for reservists, and for spouses of current Airmen in areas where base-area quality is low and unemployment is high.

Third, shift outdoor recreation resources from higher-scoring base areas to lower-scoring ones. We found that Airmen were *less* likely to use base recreation programs and services if they lived near a base area that ranked higher on the overall RAND BASE-I. It appears that, in these well-resourced areas, Airmen and their families are choosing to utilize off-base, presumably nonmilitary, resources in their communities when it comes to recreation, especially outdoor recreation. A recent study of spouses of active-duty Airmen found that roughly two-thirds (65 percent) reported participating in outdoor recreation activities, but only one-fifth of them reported doing those activities exclusively on base (Miller et al., 2011). Roughly 37 percent said they participated in outdoor activities exclusively off base, and the remaining 41 percent said they participated in outdoor recreation activities both on and off base. If program and service usage patterns

---

[48] Look-alike civilians' wives are matched to their military counterparts in terms of their age, citizenship, race, education, parental status, potential work experience, region of residence, and residential mobility in the past year (see Lim and Schulker, 2010).

can be linked to base-area quality then the Air Force may be able to redistribute unused resources to areas where usage is greater based on base-area profiles.

Fourth, consider the RAND BASE-I when selecting bases for pilot programs. For example, the Air Force has recently begun the process of revising the food services offered at on-base dining facilities. In fiscal year (FY) 2010, Air Force Services selected six pilot bases for the Food Transformation Initiative (FTI), the goal of which is to provide dining options that better match the community and mission needs. Changes include expanded menus, healthier options, and longer hours of operation at on-base dining facilities. Dining facilities will also expand their coverage, allowing civilians and families to utilize services in an effort to increase a sense of community on base. We found that Airmen who lived near base areas that score higher on the income and poverty domain of the RAND BASE-I were *more* likely to use on-base food services and report *lower* levels of base cohesion. These appear to be areas where the FTI could be piloted to see whether (1) Airman satisfaction with on-base food options increases (given that they are more likely to use the facilities) and (2) expanding the reach of dining facilities increases sense of community. At the other end of the spectrum, base areas characterized by lower scores on the income and poverty domain, where Airmen may be *less* likely to use on-base food services, may also be good pilot locations. Altering the food environment at these bases may motivate these Airmen and their families to increase utilization of food-related services. If a test program does not include both bases located in relatively well-off communities and bases located in poorer communities, the results of the test may be misleading. A test program fielded in a resource-rich community might show limited impact, but, if it had been fielded in a resource-poor community, it might have shown great promise.

Fifth, tailor the Air Force Relocation Assistance Program to accentuate areas where a base can compensate for lack of resources in the surrounding community. This may be especially relevant for bases where the surrounding area is rural or is of low SES. We found that Airmen near base areas that ranked higher on the RAND BASE-I reported greater satisfaction with a host of neighborhood resources (e.g., child care, jobs, health care). Unfortunately, this means that Airmen who lived in base areas characterized by lower scores, as rated by the RAND BASE-I and the income and poverty and employment domains, reported lower satisfaction with community resources. Similarly, Airmen who lived near base areas with higher scores on the transportation domain reported lower satisfaction with community resources. Given the positive correlation between the transportation domain and urbanicity (with higher scores more likely in more-rural areas), it appears that Airmen who live in these areas may need more information about Air Force programs and services that may bridge the gap between what they need or want and what the outside community can provide.

How Air Force Medical Service, Community Action Information Board, and
Integrated Delivery System Can Use Neighborhood and Area Quality Data

Other Air Force organizations focused on promoting the health and well-being of Airmen and their families may also find neighborhood and area data useful in more efficiently and effectively fulfilling their missions. These organizations include Air Force Medical Service and the Community Action Information Board (CAIB) and its action arm, the Integrated Delivery System (IDS). Neighborhood and area data sources, such as the RAND BASE-I, could be used to identify bases where conditions in the surrounding area may lead to increased stress and strain on Airmen and their families. As we have noted in this report, the existing literature has found that neighborhoods characterized by social disorganization are associated with worse health and well-being among residents, including both physical and mental health. Although our overall measure of base-area quality were not linked to the measures of health and well-being available to us in the Community Assessment Survey, it could be that other aspects of community, especially those associated with *perceptions* of neighborhood quality, may be important. For example, if base areas characterized by high poverty rates, high unemployment, and low annual incomes (e.g., the income and poverty and employment domains) are perceived to be less safe by residents (see Scarborough et al., 2010; Snedker, 2010), then fear of crime and victimization may be associated with worse mental health (Stafford, Chandola, and Marmot, 2007). If this is the case, then the Air Force may want to provide additional support for stress-related health care (e.g., counseling services, behavioral health care) to Airmen and their families who live in those areas. Moreover, with an eye to prevention, the Air Force might consider emphasizing resiliency programs for Airmen and their families assigned to bases located in base areas with more-stressful environments.

Another way in which the Air Force Medical Service may use neighborhood and area data is to identify areas where out-of-network, civilian providers may be more plentiful. These may be areas where the Air Force can "share" specialists within the local community and forge community partnerships. Conversely, there may also be areas where certain types of care providers are lacking, in which case Airmen and their families may not have access to out-of-network providers. The Health Resources and Services Administration (HRSA), a division of the U.S. Department of Health and Human Services, produces a website on which one can find Health Professional Shortage Areas (HPSAs) based on availability of primary care physicians, dentists, and mental health care providers (see HRSA, undated). These areas are defined by the ratio of population to clinician, among other criteria.[49] CAIBs and IDSs (Air Force level, MAJCOM level, and base level) might also find information about the relative resources of base areas to be informative in their efforts to foster collaborative partnerships with service providers and helping agencies in the community.

Our results showed that Airmen who lived in base areas that ranked higher on the overall RAND BASE-I were more satisfied with the quality and availability of health care both on and off base than their peers who lived in lower-quality base areas. Existing literature has found that lower-SES areas have fewer health care resources (Agency for Healthcare Research and Quality, 2011; Blustein, Borden, and Valentine, 2010; Rosenblatt et al., 2006) and lower-quality health care resources (Franks et al., 2003; Mehta et al., 2008; Schootman et al., 2006) than more-affluent areas. Our results corroborate this research and suggest that one piece of information that the Air Force Medical Service can use to maximize its impact and most efficiently and effectively distribute limited resources is to examine the SES of the civilian areas where Airmen and their families live.

How Installation Commanders Can Use Neighborhood and Area Quality Data

Our findings also have relevance for how installation, or base, commanders can use neighborhood and area quality data. Specifically, we found that Airmen who lived in higher-quality base areas reported *lower* levels of base cohesion. The same was true for every domain except transportation. This suggests a tension between a highly cohesive base environment and a high-quality civilian area around the base. The finding suggests that base commanders in those areas that score higher on the RAND BASE-I may need to make extra efforts to foster base cohesion and sense of community among Airmen assigned to their bases, especially those who live off base.

However, we caution that a sense of community and social cohesion on base should not come at the expense of an Airman's link to the community outside the confines of the base. Bowen and colleagues (Bowen, Martin, and Mancini, 1999; Bowen, Martin, Mancini, and Nelson, 2000, 2001; Mancini, Bowen, and Martin, 2005; Huebner et al., 2009) argue for a community capacity-building model in which the military provides support for service members and their families as does the community, through partnerships and collaborations within the existing community at large. This model acknowledges that military families do not exist in a vacuum but are embedded in a larger community context and that both formal (i.e., military) and informal (i.e., community) connections are important for family health and well-being (Huebner et al.,

---

[49] The criteria can be found at HRSA, 2003.

105

2009). Key to the model is finding ways in which formal and informal networks can reinforce one another. Ultimately, interactions of both kinds, formal and informal, should serve to increase social capital among service members and their families, providing a sense of community and trust and shared values and social norms (see Coleman, 1988; Putnam, 2000). The model does not advocate an us-versus-them (i.e., military-versus-civilian) approach in order to create social cohesion. Rather, it encourages military leadership to seek out ways in which service members can interact with fellow community members in order to create a support system in which everyone involved feels a shared responsibility to support military families.

We also encourage base commanders to think about how they can use social indicators and neighborhood studies methodologies to focus on their own local community. The methodology we used to create the RAND BASE-I is extremely flexible, allowing users to customize the indicators used to assess neighborhood base-area quality (in whatever way *neighborhood* may be defined). For example, base commanders could focus on indicators related to issues that are most relevant to the Airmen and families who are assigned to their installations (e.g., child care, recreation, employment, education). These indicators need to be available on a national level because the goal of the index would be to assess the quality and characteristics of only one geographic area. Base commanders could also create an index to reflect changing conditions in the surrounding area over time. Given recent changes in the economic climate across the country, it stands to reason that recovery (and setbacks) will take time. To assess improvement (or deterioration), base commanders may want to track long-term community quality. Finally, because change of command occurs frequently, a customized index of community quality and characteristics may provide context for command shifts, giving the incoming base commander a sort of "lay of the land."

Neighborhood and base-area characteristics also help commanders understand why their populations' needs, attitudes, or behavior may differ from others' in the same MAJCOM: Their bases' population may be facing greater temptations or greater stressors than those at other bases in the MAJCOM.

How Military Researchers Can Use Neighborhood and Area Quality Data

Neighborhood studies research is truly an interdisciplinary area. Yet we are aware of few studies in the realm of military studies that utilize the data and techniques common to neighborhood research.[50] There are existing and ongoing data sets frequently used by

---

[50] However, we are aware of studies that examine how the quality and characteristics of neighborhoods may affect service members and their families. For example, as we noted earlier, a fairly large literature has

military researchers, both military and civilian, that could easily be linked to geographically based data, such as the census. Examples include the surveys used in this study (i.e., the Community Assessment Survey and the Caring for People Survey), the Defense Manpower Data Center's Status of Forces Survey, and DoD's Millennium Cohort Study.[51] By linking these surveys to neighborhood data, or by adding questions about neighborhood to existing survey data collection, researchers can expand the explanatory power of their analyses. Understanding how and why neighborhoods may affect the health and well-being of service members and their families, their satisfaction with military life, and ultimately their retention and career decisions can be an additional consideration in how policymakers and military leadership design and implement policies affecting military members and their families.

Conclusion

This study was designed to help Air Force Services enhance its ability to adapt support for Airmen and their families through analyses of the relevance of neighborhood and area characteristics of major Air Force installations located within the United States. Using basic sociodemographic indicators from the U.S. Census Bureau, we were able to show that the quality of base areas (i.e., those areas where Airmen and their families actually live) varies. Further, those characteristics have a significant association with many important Airman outcomes (e.g., perceptions of social cohesion, satisfaction with neighborhood resources). Given this finding, the use of neighborhood characteristics can play an increased role in determining resource allocation, beyond the factors already used. We caution, however, that neighborhood and area factors are not the only additional pieces of data that should be used in the decisionmaking process. Nonetheless, increased utilization of neighborhood and geographic area characteristics in social science, military health, and resource-allocation research is something that warrants further attention.

---

examined how employment opportunities affect the careers of military spouses (e.g., Cooke and Speirs, 2005; Harrell et al., 2004; Hosek et al., 2002; Lim, Golinelli, and Cho, 2007). Other research has examined satisfaction and retention focusing on QOL issues (e.g., on-base housing, counseling services, child-care centers, fitness and recreation centers) (e.g., Hansen and Wenger, 2002a, 2002b; Harrison, Brennan, and Levine, 2000). Very little of this work focuses on aggregate, community-level neighborhood characteristics, nor does it tend to use analysis methods traditional to the fields of neighborhood studies or social indicators research.

[51] See Millennium Cohort Study, undated.

Appendix A. Distribution of Airmen, by ZIP Code

Figures A.1 and A.2 show, respectively, the distribution of active-duty and reserve Airmen, by ZIP Code. Figure 2.1 in Chapter Two shows the distribution of these two populations combined.

Figure A.1 Distribution of Active-Duty Air Force Personnel, by ZIP Code

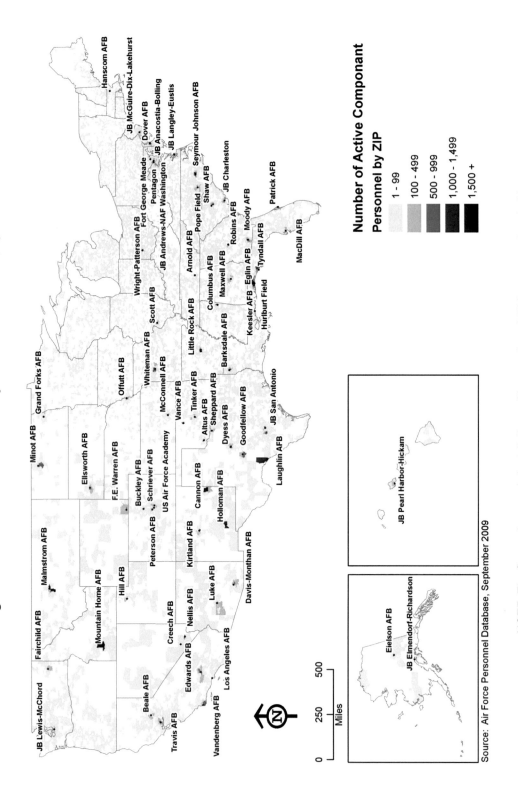

Number of Active Componant Personnel by ZIP

- 1 - 99
- 100 - 499
- 500 - 999
- 1,000 - 1,499
- 1,500 +

Source: Air Force Personnel Database, September 2009

NOTE: The figure shows only installations with more than 1,000 permanent party Airmen.

110

Figure A.2 Distribution of Reserve Air Force Personnel, by ZIP Code

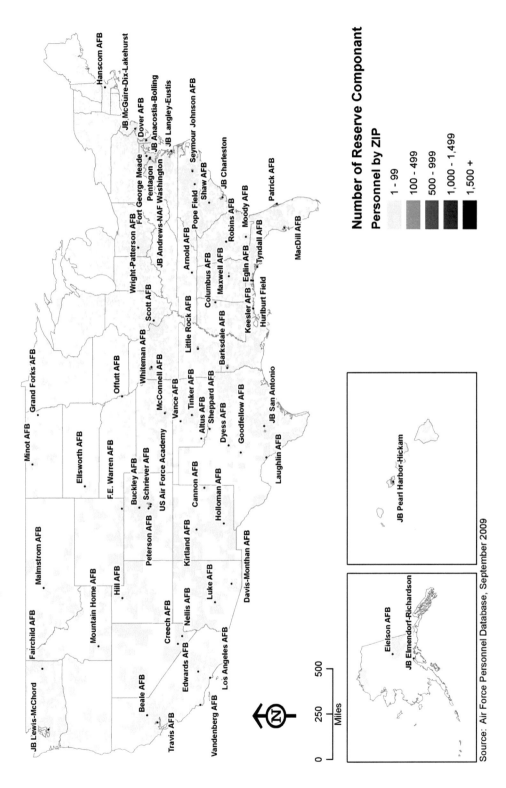

Number of Reserve Componant Personnel by ZIP

1 - 99
100 - 499
500 - 999
1,000 - 1,499
1,500 +

Source: Air Force Personnel Database, September 2009

NOTE: The figure shows only installations with more than 1,000 permanent party Airmen.

111

Appendix B. Alternative RAND Base Area Social and Economic Index Specifications

In this appendix, we present three alternative specifications of the RAND BASE-I: (1) by base-area boundary (see Table B.1), (2) by equally weighted indicator (see Table B.2), and (3) by standardizing variances (see Tables B.3 and B.4).

Table B.1
Comparison of Equally Weighted RAND Base Area Social and Economic Index Domains, by Area Boundary

Base Area	30-Minute Boundary		60-Minute Boundary		90-Minute Boundary	
	RAND BASE-I	Rank	RAND BASE-I	Rank	RAND BASE-I	Rank
Altus AFB, OK	−89.55	12	10.11	40	18.74	31
JB Anacostia-Bolling, DC	−107.45	16	59.63	3	58.77	2
JB Andrews-NAF Washington, MD	−95.06	14	55.93	7	52.13	7
Arnold AFB, TN	N/A	N/A	−8.08	56	−7.34	56
Barksdale AFB, LA	−79.33	8	4.59	48	2.30	52
Beale AFB, CA	−363.98	60	−2.75	53	−4.48	54
Buckley AFB, CO	−190.07	36	47.03	12	48.71	9
Cannon AFB, NM	−87.72	11	24.73	21	24.89	22
JB Charleston, SC	−216.29	46	−12.87	58	−21.45	60
Columbus AFB, MS	−145.13	20	−33.83	64	−30.64	64
Creech AFB, NV	N/A	N/A	20.17	27	23.58	25
Davis-Monthan AFB, AZ	−134.09	19	32.48	19	24.91	21
Dover AFB, DE	−257.37	52	1.22	50	12.99	39
Dyess AFB, TX	−178.46	33	22.09	24	18.42	32
Edwards AFB, CA	−406.60	63	−64.62	66	−104.68	66
Eglin AFB, FL	−173.69	29	9.82	41	4.37	47
Eielson AFB, AK	−289.82	56	17.40	32	17.78	33
Ellsworth AFB, SD	−156.33	23	36.78	16	36.86	17
JB Elmendorf-Richardson, AK	−372.25	61	4.69	47	2.37	51
Fairchild AFB, WA	−307.36	57	20.83	25	14.53	37
F. E. Warren AFB, WY	−29.43	5	40.12	15	45.99	13
Fort George Meade, MD	−89.74	13	58.10	4	54.16	5

113

Base Area	30-Minute Boundary RAND BASE-I	Rank	60-Minute Boundary RAND BASE-I	Rank	90-Minute Boundary RAND BASE-I	Rank
Goodfellow AFB, TX	−17.74	3	19.81	28	18.85	30
Grand Forks AFB, ND	−25.35	4	56.44	6	56.16	4
Hanscom AFB, MA	−156.90	24	41.18	14	38.70	16
Hill AFB, UT	−100.95	15	48.17	11	48.37	10
Holloman AFB, NM	−9.63	2	−28.72	63	−6.22	55
Hurlburt Field, FL	−198.99	42	0.12	51	2.27	53
Keesler AFB, MS	−311.02	58	−7.27	55	−10.33	57
Kirtland AFB, NM	−201.23	43	14.93	38	13.04	38
JB Langley-Eustis, VA	−214.88	45	24.41	22	19.40	28
Laughlin AFB, TX	−229.03	47	−38.16	65	−31.96	65
JB Lewis-McChord, WA	−337.88	59	11.74	39	15.59	35
Little Rock AFB, AR	−187.24	35	16.40	35	9.19	44
Los Angeles AFB, CA	−198.85	41	33.45	18	24.99	20
Luke AFB, AZ	−193.33	38	14.96	37	23.15	26
MacDill AFB, FL	−230.24	48	7.25	44	10.15	43
Malmstrom AFB, MT	−176.46	32	18.57	29	20.72	27
Maxwell AFB, AL	−179.99	34	−20.89	61	−29.44	63
McConnell AFB, KS	−170.39	28	44.31	13	44.98	14
JB McGuire-Dix-Lakehurst, NJ	−234.84	49	35.00	17	33.20	18
Minot AFB, ND	0.16	1	62.33	2	60.27	1
Moody AFB, GA	−158.17	26	3.46	49	−23.57	62
Mountain Home AFB, ID	−388.99	62	−1.99	52	42.83	15
Nellis AFB, NV	−196.38	40	23.01	23	24.09	23
Offutt AFB, NE	−157.88	25	52.31	9	47.62	11
Patrick AFB, FL	−151.63	21	17.73	31	11.91	41
JB Pearl Harbor–Hickam, HI	−174.83	30	24.96	20	23.79	24
Pentagon, VA	−52.14	6	62.68	1	56.56	3
Peterson AFB, CO	−122.84	18	50.25	10	47.59	12
Pope Field, NC	−176.26	31	−17.11	60	3.40	50
Robins AFB, GA	−161.40	27	−2.84	54	−19.38	59
JB San Antonio, TX	−116.41	17	16.43	34	12.02	40
Schriever AFB, CO	N/A	N/A	52.50	8	52.93	6
Scott AFB, IL	−193.54	39	15.66	36	16.14	34
Seymour Johnson AFB, NC	−212.83	44	−12.91	59	3.49	49
Shaw AFB, SC	−277.37	54	−22.21	62	−22.64	61

114

Base Area	30-Minute Boundary		60-Minute Boundary		90-Minute Boundary	
	RAND BASE-I	Rank	RAND BASE-I	Rank	RAND BASE-I	Rank
Sheppard AFB, TX	−279.23	55	5.32	46	11.43	42
Tinker AFB, OK	−151.96	22	17.22	33	14.86	36
Travis AFB, CA	−245.68	50	7.96	43	8.59	45
Tyndall AFB, FL	−85.59	9	−11.29	57	−13.49	58
U.S. Air Force Academy, CO	−58.29	7	57.84	5	49.51	8
Vance AFB, OK	−190.07	37	5.33	45	4.22	48
Vandenberg AFB, CA	−86.73	10	9.56	42	4.93	46
Whiteman AFB, MO	−254.33	51	20.78	26	29.31	19
Wright-Patterson AFB, OH	−258.61	53	17.98	30	18.95	29

NOTE: Arnold AFB, Creech AFB, and Schriever AFB do not have 30-minute RAND BASE-I scores because each contains only one census tract. State abbreviation is given in parentheses. Green text = top five base areas. Red text = bottom five base areas. The RAND BASE-I contains 20 indicators of the social and economic characteristics of the area within a 60-mile radius around a base. The Air Force cannot control these characteristics (e.g., unemployment rates, vacant-housing rates, education level of the general populace), but it can consider their potential impact on Airmen and their families. The RAND BASE-I should not be viewed as an indicator of absolute neighborhood quality or as an indicator of "most-preferred places to live."

Table B.2
Equally Weighted RAND Base Area Social and Economic Index Indicators, 60-Minute Boundary

Base Area	RAND BASE-I(I)	Base Area	RAND BASE-I(I)
Altus AFB, OK	−13.25	Little Rock AFB, AR	5.53
JB Anacostia-Bolling, DC	62.01	Los Angeles AFB, CA	27.28
JB Andrews-NAF Washington, MD	57.91	Luke AFB, AZ	5.75
Arnold AFB, TN	−18.72	MacDill AFB, FL	−0.23
Barksdale AFB, LA	−3.62	Malmstrom AFB, MT	2.06
Beale AFB, CA	−16.00	Maxwell AFB, AL	−29.75
Buckley AFB, CO	42.34	McConnell AFB, KS	34.68
Cannon AFB, NM	3.04	JB McGuire-Dix-Lakehurst, NJ	32.07
JB Charleston, SC	−23.94	Minot AFB, ND	48.38
Columbus AFB, MS	−45.85	Moody AFB, GA	−11.10
Creech AFB, NV	13.65	Mountain Home AFB, ID	−24.44
Davis-Monthan AFB, AZ	29.41	Nellis AFB, NV	14.71
Dover AFB, DE	−9.36	Offutt AFB, NE	44.51
Dyess AFB, TX	8.88	Patrick AFB, FL	8.31
Edwards AFB, CA	−101.65	JB Pearl Harbor–Hickam, HI	11.51
Eglin AFB, FL	−4.17	Pentagon, VA	64.77
Eielson AFB, AK	−8.94	Peterson AFB, CO	46.11
Ellsworth AFB, SD	20.72	Pope Field, NC	−30.44
JB Elmendorf-Richardson, AK	−12.26	Robins AFB, GA	−14.56
Fairchild AFB, WA	9.04	JB San Antonio, TX	6.88
F. E. Warren AFB, WY	31.23	Schriever AFB, CO	49.63
Fort George Meade, MD	59.29	Scott AFB, IL	9.28
Goodfellow AFB, TX	1.81	Seymour Johnson AFB, NC	−27.17
Grand Forks AFB, ND	43.11	Shaw AFB, SC	−31.28
Hanscom AFB, MA	38.45	Sheppard AFB, TX	−14.81
Hill AFB, UT	40.33	Tinker AFB, OK	4.69
Holloman AFB, NM	−56.67	Travis AFB, CA	−3.35
Hurlburt Field, FL	−18.57	Tyndall AFB, FL	−32.34
Keesler AFB, MS	−20.60	U.S. Air Force Academy, CO	55.24
Kirtland AFB, NM	0.98	Vance AFB, OK	−22.14
JB Langley-Eustis, VA	16.06	Vandenberg AFB, CA	−10.39
Laughlin AFB, TX	−63.24	Whiteman AFB, MO	11.22
JB Lewis-McChord, WA	0.09	Wright-Patterson AFB, OH	9.40

NOTE: In the RAND BASE-I(I), each of the 20 *indicators* is weighted equally. In the RAND BASE-I (presented in Table B.1 and in the main body of the report), each of the six *domains* is weighted equally. The RAND BASE-I contains 20 indicators of the social and economic characteristics of the area within a 60-mile radius around a base. The Air Force cannot control these characteristics (e.g., unemployment rates, vacant-housing rates, education level of the general populace), but it can consider their potential impact on Airmen and their families. The RAND BASE-I should not be viewed as an indicator of absolute neighborhood quality or as an indicator of "most-preferred places to live."

Standardized Variances

The key to creating an index that can be used to compare entities (e.g., people, years, geographic regions) is to scale, or standardize, indicators so that they are directly comparable across the units one wishes to compare. It is important to note that there is no one "right" way to do this. We chose a standard index formula that is frequently found in the social indicators world. Because of a reviewer's concern that our construction of the RAND BASE-I, with its range of 100 to an unconstrained negative number, may not, in actuality, be "equally weighting" the indicators because it does not constrain variances, we constructed an alternative measure of the RAND BASE-I, the RAND BASE-I(Z). For the RAND BASE-I(Z), we used the following scaling formula:

$$\frac{\text{current base} - \text{lowest-performing base}}{\text{highest-performing base}}.$$

By using what is commonly referred to as z-score transformation, we can produce a constant range from 0 to 100 on all the indicators. Table B.3 shows the correlation between the RAND BASE-I and its constituent domains and the RAND BASE-I(Z) and its constituent domains. The correlation between the RAND BASE-I and RAND BASE-I(Z) is 0.92. Domain correlations within the RAND BASE-I(Z) range between 0.58 for the employment domain and 0.99 for the income and poverty domain.

Table B.3
Correlations Between the RAND Base Area Social and Economic Index and the RAND Base Area Social and Economic Index Using z-Scores and Their Constituent Domains

RAND BASE-I Domain	RAND BASE-I(Z) Domain						
	1	2	3	4	5	6	7
1 Overall	0.92						
2 Household composition		0.73					
3 Employment			0.58				
4 Income and poverty				0.99			
5 Housing					0.88		
6 Social						0.91	
7 Transportation							0.75

Table B.4 presents the correlations between the domains within the RAND BASE-I(Z) (compared with Table 3.2 in Chapter Three, which presents the same material for the original RAND BASE-I). These correlations are generally smaller than they are in the original RAND BASE-I.

Table B.4
Correlations Between the Six Constituent Domains and the RAND Base Area Social and Economic Index Using z-Scores

RAND BASE-I Domain	RAND BASE-I(Z) Domain						
	1	2	3	4	5	6	7
1 RAND BASE-I(Z)		0.76	0.70	0.64	0.45	0.84	0.54
2 Household Composition			0.26	0.29	0.35	0.54	0.54
3 Employment				0.70	0.07	0.37	0.14
4 Income/Poverty					0.06	0.63	0.36
5 Housing						0.09	0.22
6 Social							0.36
7 Transportation							

Appendix C. Domain Scores

This appendix presents the separate results for each of the six domains that make up the RAND BASE-I: household composition, employment, income and poverty, housing, social, and transportation.

Table C.1
Household Composition Domain Results from the RAND BASE-I

Base Area	Domain Result	Base Area	Domain Result
Altus AFB, OK	47.62	Little Rock AFB, AR	21.72
JB Anacostia-Bolling, DC	61.04	Los Angeles AFB, CA	53.91
JB Andrews-NAF Washington, MD	55.23	Luke AFB, AZ	37.78
Arnold AFB, TN	24.85	MacDill AFB, FL	25.08
Barksdale AFB, LA	11.27	Malmstrom AFB, MT	51.39
Beale AFB, CA	55.20	Maxwell AFB, AL	−23.52
Buckley AFB, CO	64.46	McConnell AFB, KS	61.66
Cannon AFB, NM	72.77	JB McGuire-Dix-Lakehurst, NJ	60.00
JB Charleston, SC	−21.93	Minot AFB, ND	89.76
Columbus AFB, MS	−25.54	Moody AFB, GA	29.32
Creech AFB, NV	24.99	Mountain Home AFB, ID	46.14
Davis-Monthan AFB, AZ	48.08	Nellis AFB, NV	25.47
Dover AFB, DE	6.07	Offutt AFB, NE	70.95
Dyess AFB, TX	18.00	Patrick AFB, FL	46.84
Edwards AFB, CA	36.87	JB Pearl Harbor–Hickam, HI	42.48
Eglin AFB, FL	33.52	Pentagon, VA	63.80
Eielson AFB, AK	52.36	Peterson AFB, CO	63.60
Ellsworth AFB, SD	62.21	Pope Field, NC	−9.25
JB Elmendorf-Richardson, AK	31.86	Robins AFB, GA	8.82
Fairchild AFB, WA	51.33	JB San Antonio, TX	32.03
F. E. Warren AFB, WY	60.96	Schriever AFB, CO	62.35
Fort George Meade, MD	59.19	Scott AFB, IL	14.22
Goodfellow AFB, TX	69.89	Seymour Johnson AFB, NC	14.49
Grand Forks AFB, ND	94.86	Shaw AFB, SC	−31.75
Hanscom AFB, MA	60.50	Sheppard AFB, TX	0.52
Hill AFB, UT	72.44	Tinker AFB, OK	35.40
Holloman AFB, NM	28.39	Travis AFB, CA	44.87
Hurlburt Field, FL	27.06	Tyndall AFB, FL	9.44
Keesler AFB, MS	15.82	U.S. Air Force Academy, CO	71.91
Kirtland AFB, NM	39.46	Vance AFB, OK	32.10
JB Langley-Eustis, VA	29.37	Vandenberg AFB, CA	50.30
Laughlin AFB, TX	15.32	Whiteman AFB, MO	55.44
JB Lewis-McChord, WA	35.96	Wright-Patterson AFB, OH	31.52

NOTE: The RAND BASE-I contains 20 indicators of the social and economic characteristics of the area within a 60-mile radius around a base. The household composition domain contains two of those items: the percentage of households that are headed by women and the average household size. The Air Force cannot control these characteristics, but it can consider their potential impact on Airmen and their families. The RAND BASE-I should not be viewed as an indicator of absolute neighborhood quality or as an indicator of "most-preferred places to live."

Table C.2
Employment Domain Results from the RAND BASE-I

Base Area	Domain Result	Base Area	Domain Result
Altus AFB, OK	48.18	Little Rock AFB, AR	24.22
JB Anacostia-Bolling, DC	58.88	Los Angeles AFB, CA	10.58
JB Andrews-NAF Washington, MD	54.37	Luke AFB, AZ	9.97
Arnold AFB, TN	−53.17	MacDill AFB, FL	−20.33
Barksdale AFB, LA	−10.34	Malmstrom AFB, MT	16.00
Beale AFB, CA	−48.28	Maxwell AFB, AL	−44.65
Buckley AFB, CO	38.40	McConnell AFB, KS	48.95
Cannon AFB, NM	71.91	JB McGuire-Dix-Lakehurst, NJ	8.51
JB Charleston, SC	−18.63	Minot AFB, ND	96.73
Columbus AFB, MS	−66.26	Moody AFB, GA	14.12
Creech AFB, NV	3.63	Mountain Home AFB, ID	12.48
Davis-Monthan AFB, AZ	0.48	Nellis AFB, NV	20.27
Dover AFB, DE	6.70	Offutt AFB, NE	56.87
Dyess AFB, TX	49.17	Patrick AFB, FL	−13.24
Edwards AFB, CA	−81.99	JB Pearl Harbor–Hickam, HI	48.71
Eglin AFB, FL	3.50	Pentagon, VA	64.82
Eielson AFB, AK	58.40	Peterson AFB, CO	35.80
Ellsworth AFB, SD	57.79	Pope Field, NC	−30.89
JB Elmendorf-Richardson, AK	−3.99	Robins AFB, GA	−7.80
Fairchild AFB, WA	40.62	JB San Antonio, TX	18.57
F. E. Warren AFB, WY	−5.49	Schriever AFB, CO	34.54
Fort George Meade, MD	58.94	Scott AFB, IL	−1.18
Goodfellow AFB, TX	46.48	Seymour Johnson AFB, NC	−18.33
Grand Forks AFB, ND	78.23	Shaw AFB, SC	−54.89
Hanscom AFB, MA	15.62	Sheppard AFB, TX	60.91
Hill AFB, UT	49.09	Tinker AFB, OK	28.28
Holloman AFB, NM	−8.26	Travis AFB, CA	−14.84
Hurlburt Field, FL	6.91	Tyndall AFB, FL	11.73
Keesler AFB, MS	−14.54	U.S. Air Force Academy, CO	40.97
Kirtland AFB, NM	32.91	Vance AFB, OK	80.45
JB Langley-Eustis, VA	31.99	Vandenberg AFB, CA	28.90
Laughlin AFB, TX	−19.10	Whiteman AFB, MO	11.81
JB Lewis-McChord, WA	−3.71	Wright-Patterson AFB, OH	0.01

NOTE: The RAND BASE-I contains 20 indicators of the social and economic characteristics of the area within a 60-mile radius around a base. The Employment Domain contains two of those items: the percentage of area residents in the labor force and the percentage of area residents who are unemployed. The Air Force cannot control these characteristics, but it can consider their potential impact on Airmen and their families. The RAND BASE-I should not be viewed as an indicator of absolute neighborhood quality or as an indicator of "most-preferred places to live."

Table C.3
Income and Poverty Domain Results from the RAND BASE-I

Base Area	Domain Result	Base Area	Domain Result
Altus AFB, OK	−139.83	Little Rock AFB, AR	−82.52
JB Anacostia-Bolling, DC	76.55	Los Angeles AFB, CA	15.15
JB Andrews-NAF Washington, MD	67.34	Luke AFB, AZ	−39.02
Arnold AFB, TN	−135.13	MacDill AFB, FL	−49.37
Barksdale AFB, LA	−77.61	Malmstrom AFB, MT	−87.87
Beale AFB, CA	−133.83	Maxwell AFB, AL	−123.46
Buckley AFB, CO	5.76	McConnell AFB, KS	−48.49
Cannon AFB, NM	−58.45	JB McGuire-Dix-Lakehurst, NJ	7.67
JB Charleston, SC	−106.15	Minot AFB, ND	7.15
Columbus AFB, MS	−176.69	Moody AFB, GA	−97.39
Creech AFB, NV	8.01	Mountain Home AFB, ID	−160.69
Davis-Monthan AFB, AZ	−4.99	Nellis AFB, NV	4.09
Dover AFB, DE	−94.33	Offutt AFB, NE	−16.97
Dyess AFB, TX	−64.01	Patrick AFB, FL	−42.73
Edwards AFB, CA	−385.62	JB Pearl Harbor–Hickam, HI	−49.46
Eglin AFB, FL	−81.21	Pentagon, VA	76.98
Eielson AFB, AK	−144.78	Peterson AFB, CO	4.62
Ellsworth AFB, SD	−78.82	Pope Field, NC	−144.20
JB Elmendorf-Richardson, AK	−149.93	Robins AFB, GA	−107.87
Fairchild AFB, WA	−20.74	JB San Antonio, TX	−68.16
F. E. Warren AFB, WY	−104.66	Schriever AFB, CO	12.46
Fort George Meade, MD	56.99	Scott AFB, IL	−74.76
Goodfellow AFB, TX	−76.93	Seymour Johnson AFB, NC	−132.04
Grand Forks AFB, ND	−2.24	Shaw AFB, SC	−132.28
Hanscom AFB, MA	7.48	Sheppard AFB, TX	−148.97
Hill AFB, UT	−13.81	Tinker AFB, OK	−101.28
Holloman AFB, NM	−196.16	Travis AFB, CA	−84.00
Hurlburt Field, FL	−98.14	Tyndall AFB, FL	−86.25
Keesler AFB, MS	−142.02	U.S. Air Force Academy, CO	21.60
Kirtland AFB, NM	−102.44	Vance AFB, OK	−194.27
JB Langley-Eustis, VA	−43.63	Vandenberg AFB, CA	−81.55
Laughlin AFB, TX	−148.91	Whiteman AFB, MO	−74.61
JB Lewis-McChord, WA	−98.64	Wright-Patterson AFB, OH	−81.38

NOTE: The RAND BASE-I contains 20 indicators of the social and economic characteristics of the area within a 60-mile radius around a base. The income and poverty domain contains five of those items: median household income, mean amount of public assistance, median family income, the percentage of families in the area who are in poverty, and the percentage of female-headed households in the area that are in poverty. The Air Force cannot control these characteristics, but it can consider their potential impact on Airmen and their families. The RAND BASE-I should not be viewed as an indicator of absolute neighborhood quality or as an indicator of "most-preferred places to live."

Table C.4
Housing Domain Results from the RAND BASE-I

Base Area	Domain Result	Base Area	Domain Result
Altus AFB, OK	13.44	Little Rock AFB, AR	46.04
JB Anacostia-Bolling, DC	54.94	Los Angeles AFB, CA	−11.22
JB Andrews-NAF Washington, MD	53.56	Luke AFB, AZ	4.73
Arnold AFB, TN	52.15	MacDill AFB, FL	2.07
Barksdale AFB, LA	36.19	Malmstrom AFB, MT	−0.80
Beale AFB, CA	18.41	Maxwell AFB, AL	24.65
Buckley AFB, CO	41.52	McConnell AFB, KS	69.85
Cannon AFB, NM	13.58	JB McGuire-Dix-Lakehurst, NJ	37.04
JB Charleston, SC	−11.03	Minot AFB, ND	32.33
Columbus AFB, MS	34.00	Moody AFB, GA	33.63
Creech AFB, NV	−28.98	Mountain Home AFB, ID	8.91
Davis-Monthan AFB, AZ	33.09	Nellis AFB, NV	−27.69
Dover AFB, DE	29.81	Offutt AFB, NE	65.61
Dyess AFB, TX	27.09	Patrick AFB, FL	−5.97
Edwards AFB, CA	−46.63	JB Pearl Harbor–Hickam, HI	−11.79
Eglin AFB, FL	−18.78	Pentagon, VA	56.93
Eielson AFB, AK	−38.62	Peterson AFB, CO	49.39
Ellsworth AFB, SD	26.14	Pope Field, NC	15.25
JB Elmendorf-Richardson, AK	17.34	Robins AFB, GA	30.37
Fairchild AFB, WA	27.86	JB San Antonio, TX	37.47
F. E. Warren AFB, WY	47.82	Schriever AFB, CO	54.40
Fort George Meade, MD	63.42	Scott AFB, IL	51.08
Goodfellow AFB, TX	41.19	Seymour Johnson AFB, NC	29.76
Grand Forks AFB, ND	40.57	Shaw AFB, SC	21.53
Hanscom AFB, MA	46.81	Sheppard AFB, TX	22.75
Hill AFB, UT	56.05	Tinker AFB, OK	50.63
Holloman AFB, NM	−48.45	Travis AFB, CA	5.84
Hurlburt Field, FL	−62.49	Tyndall AFB, FL	−90.18
Keesler AFB, MS	37.13	U.S. Air Force Academy, CO	58.22
Kirtland AFB, NM	31.20	Vance AFB, OK	31.49
JB Langley-Eustis, VA	37.80	Vandenberg AFB, CA	−26.60
Laughlin AFB, TX	−43.18	Whiteman AFB, MO	60.53
JB Lewis-McChord, WA	15.23	Wright-Patterson AFB, OH	53.24

NOTE: The RAND BASE-I contains 20 indicators of the social and economic characteristics of the area within a 60-mile radius around a base. The housing domain contains five of those items: the percentage of area residents spending 35 percent or more of their income on rent or housing costs (these are two separate indicators), the percentage of housing units that are vacant, the percentage of housing units occupied by renters, and the percentage living in the same house since the previous year. The Air Force cannot control these characteristics, but it can consider their potential impact on Airmen and their families. The RAND BASE-I should not be viewed as an indicator of absolute neighborhood quality or as an indicator of "most-preferred places to live."

Table C.5
Social Domain Results from the RAND BASE-I

Base Area	Domain Result	Base Area	Domain Result
Altus AFB, OK	−3.57	Little Rock AFB, AR	11.60
JB Anacostia-Bolling, DC	65.03	Los Angeles AFB, CA	66.16
JB Andrews-NAF Washington, MD	62.20	Luke AFB, AZ	19.13
Arnold AFB, TN	−14.22	MacDill AFB, FL	25.13
Barksdale AFB, LA	−1.59	Malmstrom AFB, MT	42.18
Beale AFB, CA	29.58	Maxwell AFB, AL	−23.93
Buckley AFB, CO	70.37	McConnell AFB, KS	48.89
Cannon AFB, NM	−50.68	JB McGuire-Dix-Lakehurst, NJ	43.61
JB Charleston, SC	13.63	Minot AFB, ND	50.53
Columbus AFB, MS	−41.42	Moody AFB, GA	−36.13
Creech AFB, NV	46.94	Mountain Home AFB, ID	−4.74
Davis-Monthan AFB, AZ	57.07	Nellis AFB, NV	44.45
Dover AFB, DE	−4.14	Offutt AFB, NE	58.27
Dyess AFB, TX	11.60	Patrick AFB, FL	49.71
Edwards AFB, CA	19.63	JB Pearl Harbor–Hickam, HI	57.18
Eglin AFB, FL	50.95	Pentagon, VA	70.71
Eielson AFB, AK	81.29	Peterson AFB, CO	78.58
Ellsworth AFB, SD	65.50	Pope Field, NC	−8.30
JB Elmendorf-Richardson, AK	48.11	Robins AFB, GA	−12.32
Fairchild AFB, WA	60.94	JB San Antonio, TX	16.32
F. E. Warren AFB, WY	50.68	Schriever AFB, CO	81.02
Fort George Meade, MD	63.68	Scott AFB, IL	34.36
Goodfellow AFB, TX	−47.21	Seymour Johnson AFB, NC	−40.81
Grand Forks AFB, ND	34.96	Shaw AFB, SC	−13.45
Hanscom AFB, MA	55.96	Sheppard AFB, TX	9.27
Hill AFB, UT	50.97	Tinker AFB, OK	19.57
Holloman AFB, NM	−27.44	Travis AFB, CA	36.00
Hurlburt Field, FL	54.51	Tyndall AFB, FL	9.04
Keesler AFB, MS	−5.10	U.S. Air Force Academy, CO	85.63
Kirtland AFB, NM	27.07	Vance AFB, OK	−9.18
JB Langley-Eustis, VA	22.81	Vandenberg AFB, CA	0.94
Laughlin AFB, TX	−115.29	Whiteman AFB, MO	8.64
JB Lewis-McChord, WA	55.62	Wright-Patterson AFB, OH	28.34

NOTE: The RAND BASE-I contains 20 indicators of the social and economic characteristics of the area within a 60-mile radius around a base. The social domain contains four of those items: the percentage of area residents with less than a high school degree, the percentage with a bachelor's degree or more, the percentage who are currently married, and the percentage who are veterans. The Air Force cannot control these characteristics, but it can consider their potential impact on Airmen and their families. The RAND BASE-I should not be viewed as an indicator of absolute neighborhood quality or as an indicator of "most-preferred places to live."

Table C.6
Transportation Domain Results from the RAND BASE-I

Base Area	Domain Result	Base Area	Domain Result
Altus AFB, OK	94.85	Little Rock AFB, AR	77.33
JB Anacostia-Bolling, DC	41.36	Los Angeles AFB, CA	66.11
JB Andrews-NAF Washington, MD	42.87	Luke AFB, AZ	57.18
Arnold AFB, TN	77.01	MacDill AFB, FL	60.91
Barksdale AFB, LA	69.65	Malmstrom AFB, MT	90.53
Beale AFB, CA	62.44	Maxwell AFB, AL	65.56
Buckley AFB, CO	61.64	McConnell AFB, KS	85.01
Cannon AFB, NM	99.26	JB McGuire-Dix-Lakehurst, NJ	53.20
JB Charleston, SC	66.91	Minot AFB, ND	97.49
Columbus AFB, MS	72.89	Moody AFB, GA	77.19
Creech AFB, NV	66.42	Mountain Home AFB, ID	85.96
Davis-Monthan AFB, AZ	61.14	Nellis AFB, NV	71.48
Dover AFB, DE	63.20	Offutt AFB, NE	79.11
Dyess AFB, TX	90.69	Patrick AFB, FL	71.77
Edwards AFB, CA	70.03	JB Pearl Harbor–Hickam, HI	62.68
Eglin AFB, FL	71.92	Pentagon, VA	42.83
Eielson AFB, AK	95.77	Peterson AFB, CO	69.49
Ellsworth AFB, SD	87.83	Pope Field, NC	74.71
JB Elmendorf-Richardson, AK	84.75	Robins AFB, GA	71.78
Fairchild AFB, WA	80.70	JB San Antonio, TX	62.34
F. E. Warren AFB, WY	75.70	Schriever AFB, CO	70.20
Fort George Meade, MD	46.36	Scott AFB, IL	70.21
Goodfellow AFB, TX	85.46	Seymour Johnson AFB, NC	69.47
Grand Forks AFB, ND	92.24	Shaw AFB, SC	77.61
Hanscom AFB, MA	60.68	Sheppard AFB, TX	87.47
Hill AFB, UT	74.27	Tinker AFB, OK	70.71
Holloman AFB, NM	79.63	Travis AFB, CA	59.86
Hurlburt Field, FL	72.90	Tyndall AFB, FL	78.47
Keesler AFB, MS	65.11	U.S. Air Force Academy, CO	68.74
Kirtland AFB, NM	61.39	Vance AFB, OK	91.38
JB Langley-Eustis, VA	68.12	Vandenberg AFB, CA	85.35
Laughlin AFB, TX	82.22	Whiteman AFB, MO	62.86
JB Lewis-McChord, WA	65.96	Wright-Patterson AFB, OH	76.14

NOTE: The RAND BASE-I contains 20 indicators of the social and economic characteristics of the area within a 60-mile radius around a base. The transportation domain contains two of those items: mean travel time to work and the percentage with access to at least one automobile. The Air Force cannot control these characteristics, but it can consider their potential impact on Airmen and their families. The RAND BASE-I should not be viewed as an indicator of absolute neighborhood quality or as an indicator of "most-preferred places to live."

Appendix D. Detailed Results for Chapter Four, the Community Assessment Survey

This appendix provides additional detail from the analyses of the Community Assessment Survey. Tables D.1–D.4 display the distance the survey respondents live from their assigned base and descriptive statistics for the survey samples, for both active-duty and reserve Airmen. We also provide an overview of the modeling strategy and present a summary of the overall multilevel model results (see Table D.5). For those interested in the effect sizes of the significant coefficients and significant interaction terms from the survey results, we present that information for the RAND BASE-I and each domain (see Tables D.6 and D.7).

Table D.1

Distance from Assigned Base Among Survey Respondents from the Community Assessment Survey Included in Analysis, Active Duty Only

	Percentage of Survey Respondents		
Base Area	Fewer Than 10 Miles	Between 10 and 20 Miles	20+ Miles
All base areas	71.0	19.5	9.6
Altus, OK	96.1	2.8	1.1
JB Anacostia-Bolling, DC	53.8	20.5	25.7
JB Andrews-NAF Washington, MD	50.9	23.4	25.8
Barksdale AFB, LA	85.2	11.7	3.1
Beale AFB, CA	51.5	24.7	23.9
Buckley AFB, CO	76.9	13.2	9.8
Cannon AFB, NM	63.3	34.1	2.6
JB Charleston, SC	68.5	25.8	5.8
Columbus AFB, MS	88.5	8.9	2.6
Creech AFB, NV	25.9	0.4	73.7
Davis-Monthan AFB, AZ	70.7	18.0	11.3
Dover AFB, DE	86.1	10.8	3.2
Dyess AFB, TX	80.4	17.4	2.1
Edwards AFB, CA	50.1	15.4	34.5
Eglin AFB, FL	63.9	14.8	21.3
Eielson AFB, AK	76.4	21.4	2.2
Ellsworth AFB, SD	71.4	22.7	5.9

Base Area	Percentage of Survey Respondents		
	Fewer Than 10 Miles	Between 10 and 20 Miles	20+ Miles
JB Elmendorf-Richardson, AK	77.4	16.2	6.4
Fairchild AFB, WA	73.0	19.6	7.4
F. E. Warren AFB, WY	87.0	6.8	6.2
Fort George Meade, MD	67.8	17.4	14.8
Goodfellow AFB, TX	90.4	9.1	0.5
Grand Forks AFB, ND	70.2	18.6	11.2
Hanscom AFB, MA	63.4	22.3	14.3
Hill AFB, UT	89.4	8.0	2.6
Holloman AFB, NM	72.4	23.1	4.5
Hurlburt Field, FL	63.6	27.4	9.1
Keesler AFB, MS	74.5	20.5	4.9
Kirtland AFB, NM	67.0	16.4	16.6
JB Langley-Eustis, VA	77.0	16.6	6.5
Laughlin, TX	88.4	11.1	0.6
JB Lewis-McChord, WA	63.3	24.5	12.2
Little Rock (AR)	64.2	28.6	7.2
Los Angeles, CA	75.8	12.3	11.9
Luke, AZ	75.8	19.7	4.5
MacDill, FL	54.8	15.9	29.3
Malmstrom, MT	94.3	4.2	1.5
Maxwell, AL	55.4	35.5	9.1
McConnell, AL	85.6	12.6	1.8
JB McGuire-Dix-Lakehurst, NJ	65.0	18.0	16.9
Minot, ND	64.7	31.3	3.9
Moody, GA	80.2	16.8	2.9
Mountain Home, ID	55.7	34.9	9.4
Nellis, NV	70.2	21.8	8.0
Offutt, NE	85.7	11.4	3.0
Patrick, FL	63.8	22.7	13.5
JB Pearl Harbor–Hickam, HI	77.1	19.1	3.9
Pentagon, VA	46.1	26.0	27.9
Peterson, CO	69.3	24.0	6.7
Pope Field, NC	53.2	32.3	14.5
Robins, GA	78.0	16.7	5.3
JB San Antonio, TX	50.7	32.6	16.7
Schriever, CO	44.2	41.7	14.1

Base Area	Percentage of Survey Respondents		
	Fewer Than 10 Miles	Between 10 and 20 Miles	20+ Miles
Scott, IL	82.6	12.1	5.3
Seymour Johnson, NC	70.5	22.5	6.9
Shaw, SC	77.6	12.9	9.5
Sheppard, TX	78.7	19.4	2.0
Tinker, OK	68.6	20.9	10.5
Travis, CA	81.8	10.6	7.6
Tyndall, FL	72.0	22.0	6.0
U.S. Air Force Academy, CO	82.1	14.7	3.3
Vance, OK	95.9	3.6	0.6
Vandenberg, CA	74.0	21.6	4.4
Whiteman, MO	75.3	18.7	6.0
Wright-Patterson, OH	76.8	16.3	6.9

Table D.2
Distance from Assigned Base Among Survey Respondents from the Community Assessment Survey Included in the Analysis, Reserve Only

Base Area	Percentage of Survey Respondents	
	50 or Fewer Miles	50+ Miles
All base areas	67.4	32.6
Altus, OK	50.0	50.0
JB Anacostia-Bolling, DC	69.7	30.3
JB Andrews-NAF Washington, MD	65.8	34.2
Barksdale AFB, LA	70.6	29.4
Beale AFB, CA	53.3	46.7
Buckley AFB, CO	62.7	37.3
Cannon AFB, NM	50.0	50.0
JB Charleston, SC	62.2	37.8
Columbus AFB, MS	90.9	9.1
Creech AFB, NV	47.8	52.2
Davis-Monthan AFB, AZ	77.9	22.1
Dover AFB, DE	61.3	38.7
Dyess AFB, TX	100.0	0.0
Edwards AFB, CA	52.6	47.4
Eglin AFB, FL	85.7	14.3
Ellsworth AFB, SD	33.3	66.7
JB Elmendorf-Richardson, AK	75.9	24.1

	Percentage of Survey Respondents	
Base Area	50 or Fewer Miles	50+ Miles
Fairchild AFB, WA	66.7	33.3
F. E. Warren AFB, WY	57.1	42.9
Fort George Meade, MD	65.8	34.2
Goodfellow AFB, TX	0.0	100.0
Grand Forks AFB, ND	50.0	50.0
Hanscom AFB, MA	80.8	19.2
Hill AFB, UT	81.3	18.7
Holloman AFB, NM	73.3	26.7
Hurlburt Field, FL	80.3	19.7
Keesler AFB, MS	56.3	43.7
Kirtland AFB, NM	67.9	32.1
JB Langley-Eustis, VA	54.2	45.8
Laughlin AFB, TX	50.0	50.0
JB Lewis-McChord, WA	75.9	24.1
Little Rock AFB, AR	63.6	36.4
Los Angeles AFB, CA	69.4	30.6
Luke AFB, AZ	79.1	20.9
MacDill AFB, FL	73.3	26.7
Malmstrom AFB, MT	50.0	50.0
Maxwell AFB, AL	61.7	38.3
McConnell AFB, KS	77.7	22.3
JB McGuire-Dix-Lakehurst, NJ	54.5	45.5
Minot AFB, ND	0.0	100.0
Moody AFB, GA	67.7	32.3
Mountain Home AFB, ID	33.3	66.7
Nellis AFB, NV	83.0	17.1
Offutt AFB, NE	67.4	32.7
Patrick AFB, FL	68.2	31.8
JB Pearl Harbor–Hickam, HI	83.3	16.7
Pentagon, VA	62.8	37.2
Peterson AFB, CO	72.5	27.5
Pope Field, NC	63.9	36.1
Robins AFB, GA	70.7	29.3
JB San Antonio, TX	76.2	23.8
Schriever AFB, CO	81.1	18.9
Scott AFB, IL	63.1	36.9

	Percentage of Survey Respondents	
Base Area	50 or Fewer Miles	50+ Miles
Seymour Johnson AFB, NC	55.8	44.2
Shaw AFB, SC	26.7	73.3
Sheppard AFB, TX	72.7	27.3
Tinker AFB, OK	77.9	22.1
Travis AFB, CA	62.8	37.2
Tyndall AFB, FL	26.9	73.1
U.S. Air Force Academy, CO	78.6	21.4
Vance AFB, OK	55.0	45.0
Vandenberg AFB, CA	46.4	53.6
Whiteman AFB, MO	59.9	40.2

Table D.3
Descriptive Statistics from the Community Assessment Survey: Active Duty Only

Statistic	Overall	On Base	Off Base
Male (%)	77.4	82.2	75.7
Age category (%)			
18–20	23.3	1.1	10.3
21–25	41.3	19.8	33.2
26–35	26.9	43.9	33.5
36–45	4.7	29.7	18.7
46–55	0.3	4.9	3.9
55+	3.5	0.3	0.3
Marital status (%)			
Cohabiting (not married)	8.8	10.1	8.4
Divorced, separated, or widowed	3.4	2.7	6.6
Married	63.5	64.6	63.1
Never married	24.3	22.7	24.8
Dual military couple (%)	12.6	14.4	7.2
Children (%)			
Has one child	19.0	19.2	17.9
Has two children	21.2	20.6	22.1
Has three children	8.3	7.8	9.3
Has four or more children	3.3	3.1	3.8
Has child under age 6	24.6	23.4	28.0
EFMP or SNIAC family member (%)	8.5	9.1	8.3

Statistic	Overall	On Base	Off Base
Officer (%)	26.9	16.9	30.5
Rank (%)			
E1–E4	23.2	43.4	16.1
E5–E6	35.0	29.0	37.2
E7–E9	14.1	10.1	15.5
O1–O3	14.2	8.6	16.2
O4 and above	12.8	8.3	14.4
Years of service (standard deviation in parentheses)	11.3 (7.3)	9.1 (7.5)	12.1 (7.0)
Currently deployed (%)	6.6	6.1	6.8
Time at base, in months (standard deviation in parentheses)	2.9 (2.4)	2.3 (1.8)	3.1 (2.6)
Distance from base (%)			
<10 miles	71.0	N/A	60.7
>10 miles	29.0	N/A	39.3
Current residence (%)			
On base	26.1	N/A	N/A
Off base	73.9	N/A	N/A
Own home	N/A	N/A	46.2
Rent home	N/A	N/A	50.4
Government housing	N/A	N/A	3.4
Self-rated coping (standard deviation in parentheses)[a]	5.46 (1.23)	5.45 (1.27)	5.47 (1.22)
CD-RISC 2[b]	4.2 (0.63)	4.2 (0.66)	4.2 (0.62)

[a] Seven-point scale from "extremely poorly" (1) to "extremely well" (7).
[b] Average of ten items rated on a five-point scale from "not at all true" (1) to "true nearly all the time" (5).
NOTE: Means are reported. Numbers in parentheses are standard deviations.

Table D.4
Descriptive Statistics from the Community Assessment Survey: Reserve Only

Statistic	Respondents
Male (%)	73.0
Age category (%)	
18–20	1.2
21–25	4.8
26–35	24.5
36–45	36.8

Statistic	Respondents
46–55	29.0
Over 55	3.7
Marital status (%)	
Married	67.1
Cohabiting (not married)	7.7
Divorced, separated, or widowed	3.3
Never married	21.9
Dual military couple (%)	9.3
Children (%)	
Has one child	21.3
Has two children	24.2
Has three children	9.4
Has four or more children	4.7
Has child under age 6	18.3
EFMP or SNIAC family member (%)	4.5
Officer (%)	29.7
Rank (%)	
E1–E4	8.9
E5–E6	30.9
E7–E9	29.5
O1–O3	5.3
O4 and above	24.4
Years of service (standard deviation in parentheses)	18.0 (8.35)
Currently deployed (%)	3.3
Distance from base (%)	
<50 miles	67.4
>50 miles	32.6
Self-rated coping[a]	5.6 (1.09)
CD-RISC 2[b]	4.3 (0.59)

[a] Seven-point scale from "extremely poorly" (1) to "extremely well" (7).
[b] CD-RISC 2. Average of ten items rated on a five-point scale from "not at all true" (1) to "true nearly all the time" (5).
NOTE: Means are reported. Numbers in parentheses are standard deviations.

Modeling Strategy

For each RAND BASE-I or domain/outcome combination, we ran three different models: (1) a base model that includes the RAND BASE-I or domain regressed on the outcome (note that each domain is entered independently, without controlling for the other five constituent domains), (2) a model that includes all of the sample characteristics as controls,[52] and (3) a model that includes the controls and an interaction between the RAND BASE-I or domain and an indicator for whether an Airman lives on base. If the interaction was significant, we then ran separate models for Airmen who live in the civilian community (i.e., off base) and those who live in the military community (i.e., on base). Obviously, the interaction model is not applicable to reserve Airmen.

Table D.5 summarizes the results. Outcomes are listed in the rows, while the RAND BASE-I and each of the six domains are listed in the columns. The base model, with no controls, is indicated in the "B" column, the model with control is indicated by a "C," and the model with the interaction is indicated by an "I." In each cell, we indicate whether the association between the RAND BASE-I or domain and the outcome was statistically significant and whether the association was positive or negative. In the cells for the interaction model, the first row indicates whether or not the overall interaction is significant. If it was, we then ran separate models for Airmen who live on base and those who live off base, in the civilian community. Based on those models, a "yes" in the cell indicates that the RAND BASE-I or domain coefficient for living off base is larger than the coefficient for living on base. A "no" in the cell indicates that, although the interaction term is itself significant, the coefficient for living off base (from the separate models for Airmen living off base) is not larger than the coefficient for living on base (again, from the separate model for Airmen living on base).[53]

---

[52] For active-duty Airmen, the control variables include gender, age, marital status, dual military couple, number of children, EFMP or SNIAC family member, rank, years of service, currently deployed, time at current base, distance from current base, self-rated coping, and the CD-RISC 2. Control variables for reserve Airmen are the same except for time at current base, which is not available in the survey data. All control variables occur at the individual level. That is, no base-level control variables (e.g., region, population density) are included.

[53] In some cases, the interaction was statistically significant but the RAND BASE-I domain coefficients for on- and off-base Airmen were in opposite directions. Because this does not support our hypothesis that base-area associations with outcomes are stronger for Airmen who live off base, these cases also receive a "no" in the appropriate cell.

Table D.5
Summary of the Multilevel Model Results from the Community Assessment Survey

Outcome		RAND BASE-I			Household Composition			Employment			Income and Poverty			Housing			Social			Transportation		
		B	C	I	B	C	I	B	C	I	B	C	I	B	C	I	B	C	I	B	C	I
Health and well-being																						
Exercise frequency	Active duty	N*					—	N†			N†			N**	N*							
	Reserve			—						—												
Self-rated health	Active duty	N*			N*	N*	—			—			—			—			—			No*
	Reserve			—																		
Depressive symptoms	Active duty				P*	P*	—	P**	P†	—			—			—			—	P*	P*	—
	Reserve			—																		
Social support, integration, and cohesion																						
Base social cohesion[a]	Active duty	N***	N***		N***	N***		N*	N**		N***	N***		N**	N**		N*	N*	Yes*	P*	P*	
Neighborhood social cohesion	Active duty			No*	N*	N†				Yes†	N*	N*	Yes***	P*	P*		N**	N*	No**			
	Reserve			—	N*	N*																
Airman community engagement scale	Active duty	N*	N*				—		N†		N*	N*		N*	N†				—			
	Reserve	N*	N*		N†	N*																
Neighborhood social support	Active duty	N***	N**	—	P*	P*		N**	N*	Yes*	N***	N***	Yes***	N*	N**		N*	N†		P***	P***	Yes*
	Reserve										N†	N**		P†	P					P*	P***	
Community safety	Active duty	P*	P*	Yes***				P*	P*	Yes***						Yes***	P†	P†	Yes***	P*	P*	P†, No

135

Outcome		RAND BASE-I			Household Composition			Employment			Income and Poverty			Housing			Social			Transportation		
		B	C	I	B	C	I	B	C	I	B	C	I	B	C	I	B	C	I	B	C	I
Child safety	Reserve			—										P†	P*	—			—			—
	Active duty		P*	Yes†									No**	P*	P**							No*
Support for youth	Active duty			—			—			—						—			—			—
Community resource scale (overall)[a]	Active duty	P*	P*	Yes**							P**	P**		P*	P*	Yes***	P***	P***	Yes***	N***	N***	Yes***
Housing subscale[a]	Active duty	P**	P**				Yes***			No*	P**		No**			No*	P**	P**	Yes***	N**	N**	Yes***
Health care subscale[a]	Active duty	P**	P**	Yes*						Yes***	P**	P**		P*	P*		P***	P***	Yes***	N**	N**	Yes***
Child-care subscale[a]	Active duty	P**	P†								P**	P*		P*	P***	Yes***	P**	P*		N***	N***	Yes*
Job subscale[a]	Active duty	P***	P***	Yes**			Yes*	P†	P*		P***	P***	Yes***	P***	P***		P***	P***	Yes*	N***	N***	
Transportation subscale[a]	Active duty	P*	P*	Yes**							P**	P**	Yes**	P**	P**		P***	P***	Yes***	N***	N***	
Child activity subscale[a]	Active duty	P***	P***	Yes***			Yes**			Yes*	P***	P***	Yes***	P***	P***	Yes**	P***	P***	Yes***	N***	N***	Yes***
School quality	Active duty	P***	P***	Yes*	P**	P***		P**	P**		P**	P***	Yes**	P***	P***		P***	P***	Yes***	N***	N***	No***
	Reserve	P***	P***	—	P*	P**							—	P***	P***		P**	P**				
Child-care spending	Active duty	P***	P***		P***	P***		P†	P*		P***	P***		P***	P***		P***	P***		N***	N***	
	Reserve	P*		—							P***	P†					P**	P**		N***	N**	
Economic stress scale	Active duty	N†	N*								N**	N**					P**	N**	No*	N**	P*	
	Reserve			—							P***	P†					P**	P*				
Financial stress[b]	Reserve			—			—			—			—			—	N**	N**		P***	P*	—

136

Outcome		RAND BASE-I			Household Composition			Employment			Income and Poverty			Housing			Social			Transportation		
		B	C	I	B	C	I	B	C	I	B	C	I	B	C	I	B	C	I	B	C	I
Satisfaction																						
With base assignment	Active duty			—			No*										P***	P***	Yes**	N***	N***	Yes*
	Reserve	P***	P†	—			—										P**	P**	—	P**	P**	—
With Air Force way of life	Active duty			—	N†	N†	Yes***			Yes*							P***	P***	Yes***	N***	N***	Yes*
	Reserve			—			—			—							P***	P***	—	P**	P**	—
With community	Active duty	P***	P***	—	P*	P*	—				P**	P*	—	P*	P*	—	P***	P***	Yes***			
	Reserve	P**	P**	—			—	P*	P*	—	P†	P†	—	P†	P†	—	P***	P***	—			
Career																						
Career intentions	Active duty					P*					P*		—	N†		—						
	Reserve			—																		
Employer support[b]	Reserve	N*	N**	—			—	N*	N*	—	N*	N**	—			—			—			—
Employer support during deployment[b]	Reserve			—			—			—			—			—			—			—

[a] Asked of active-duty Airmen only.
[b] Asked of reserve Airmen only.

NOTE: B = bivariate association. C = controls included. I = interaction with living on base. N = negative association. P = positive association. † = p < 0.10. * = p < 0.05. ** = p < 0.01. *** = p < 0.001. In cells in the I columns, the first row indicates significance; if the interaction is significant, separate models were estimated for Airmen who live on and off base. Yes = coefficient for living off base is statistically significantly larger than the coefficient for living on base. No = coefficient for living off base is not statistically significantly larger than the coefficient for living on base or the coefficients are in opposite directions. For active-duty Airmen, the control variables include gender, age, marital status, dual military couple, number of children, EFMP or SNIAC family member, rank, years of service, currently deployed, time at current base, distance from current base, self-rated coping, and the CD-RISC 2. Control variables for reserve Airmen are the same except for time at current base, which is not available in the survey data.

Effect Sizes

As we note in Chapter Five, we opted to present results in terms of statistical significance (i.e., the outcomes that showed a statistical association with the RAND BASE-I and its constituent domains). However, statistical significance does not necessarily indicate practical significance. In the tables that follow, we provide effect sizes in order to give the reader a sense of the magnitude of the association between base-area characteristics and Airman outcomes.

Effect sizes for only the significant coefficients from Table D.5 (for the full model with controls) are shown in Table D.6. For continuous variables, effect sizes are calculated by standardizing the entire sample by one whole sample standard deviation (i.e., the standard deviation for the sample as a whole) for both predictor and outcome. For example, the effect size for the social domain's association with Airman satisfaction of their community among active-duty Airmen is 0.20. A one–standard deviation change on the social domain score results in a 0.20–standard deviation increase in life community satisfaction ratings.

Effect sizes for categorical outcomes are calculated by taking the change in probability of the outcome switching from "no" to "yes" if the predictor variable changes by one standard deviation and the outcome had a 0.5 probability of occurring before the change. There is only one categorical outcome in the analysis of the Community Assessment Survey data: career intentions. The effect size for the household composition domain's association with career intentions among active-duty Airmen is 0.01. A one–standard deviation change in household composition domain scores is associated with an increase of an active-duty respondent indicating that he or she intends to remain in the Air Force until retirement from 50 percent to 51 percent.

Table D.7 provides effect sizes for only the significant interaction terms from Table D.5. They can be interpreted in the same manner as in Table D.6.

Table D.6

Effect Sizes for Significant Coefficients from the Community Assessment Survey Results

Outcome		RAND BASE-I	Household Composition	Employment	Income and Poverty	Housing	Social	Transportation
Health and well-being								
Exercise frequency	Active duty					−0.04		
	Reserve							
Self-rated health	Active duty		−0.02					
	Reserve							
Depressive symptoms	Active duty		0.02	0.02				0.02
	Reserve							
Social support, integration, and cohesion								
Base social cohesion[a]	Active duty	−0.06	−0.06	−0.05	−0.05	−0.04	−0.03	
Neighborhood social cohesion	Active duty				−0.06			
	Reserve	−0.05	−0.04	−0.05		0.06	−0.05	0.05
Airman community engagement scale	Active duty	−0.08	−0.03		−0.05			
	Reserve	−0.08	−0.05	−0.07	−0.10	−0.02		0.08
Neighborhood social support	Active duty				−0.03	−0.05		0.05
	Reserve							0.06
Community safety	Active duty	0.05	0.05	0.06		0.06	0.04	
	Reserve					0.04		

139

Outcome		RAND BASE-I	Household Composition	Employment	Income and Poverty	Housing	Social	Transportation
Child safety	Active duty					0.07		
	Reserve							
Support for youth	Active duty							
Community resource scale (overall)[a]	Active duty	0.08			0.09	0.09	0.13	−0.14
Housing subscale[a]	Active duty						0.09	−0.11
Health care subscale[a]	Active duty	0.08			0.08	0.07	0.11	−0.08
Child-care subscale[a]	Active duty	0.03			0.03	0.09	0.04	−0.05
Jobs subscale[a]	Active duty	0.10		0.04	0.09	0.07	0.13	−0.09
Transportation subscale[a]	Active duty	0.07			0.08	0.08	0.10	−0.15
Child activity subscale[a]	Active duty	0.10			0.10	0.09	0.14	−0.14
School quality	Active duty	0.09	0.09	0.09	0.11	0.10	0.09	
	Reserve	0.10	0.10	0.11	0.10	0.11	0.11	
Child-care spending	Active duty	0.09	0.08	0.05	0.08		0.09	−0.09
	Reserve				0.10		0.10	−0.18
Economic stress scale	Active duty	−0.02			−0.02		−0.02	0.01
	Reserve							
Financial stress[b]	Reserve						−0.08	

Outcome		RAND BASE-I	Household Composition	Employment	Income and Poverty	Housing	Social	Transportation
Satisfaction								
Satisfaction with base assignment	Active duty						0.12	–0.12
	Reserve						0.08	
Satisfaction with Air Force way of life	Active duty		–0.03				0.03	–0.05
	Reserve							0.07
Satisfaction with community	Active duty	0.15	0.04		0.12	0.11	0.20	
	Reserve	0.15		0.12	0.08	0.09	0.18	
Career								
Career intentions	Active duty		0.01					
	Reserve	–0.07						
Employer support[b]	Reserve			–0.06	–0.07			0.08
Employer support during deployment[b]	Reserve							

[a] Asked only of active-duty Airmen.
[b] Asked only of reserve Airmen.
NOTE: Table contains effect sizes based on only the significant associations in the "C" Column from Table D.5 (i.e., the model with full controls). Effect sizes calculated at the individual level (versus the base level).

141

Table D.7
Effect Sizes for Significant Interaction Terms from the Caring for People Survey Results

Outcome		RAND BASE-I	Household Composition	Employment	Income and Poverty	Housing	Social	Transportation
Health and well-being								
Exercise frequency	Off base							
	On base							
Self-rated health	Off base							
	On base							
Depressive symptoms	Off base							
	On base							
Social support, integration, and cohesion								
Base social cohesion[a]	Off base						−0.03	
	On base						−0.04	
Neighborhood social cohesion	Off base			0.02	−0.02			
	On base			0.00	−0.01			
Airman community engagement scale	Off base							
	On base							
Neighborhood social support	Off base			0.02				0.06
	On base			−0.01				0.03
Community safety	Off base	0.08		0.07	0.04	0.08	0.07	
	On base	0.00		0.02	−0.05	0.00	0.00	
Child safety	Off base	0.03						
	On base	0.00						
Support for youth	Off base							

Outcome		RAND BASE-I	Household Composition	Employment	Income and Poverty	Housing	Social	Transportation
	On base							
Community resource scale (overall)[a]	Off base	−0.03			0.10	0.11	0.15	−0.09
	On base	−0.01			0.05	0.05	0.08	−0.04
Housing subscale[a]	Off base		0.07	−0.07			0.10	−0.15
	On base		0.01	−0.01			0.07	−0.03
Health care subscale[a]	Off base	0.08					0.13	−0.09
	On base	0.05					0.06	−0.05
Child-care subscale[a]	Off base					0.07		−0.06
	On base					0.02		−0.03
Job subscale[a]	Off base		0.14		0.09		0.06	
	On base		0.11		0.07		0.03	
Transportation subscale[a]	Off base	0.12			0.08			
	On base	0.07			0.06			
Child activity subscale[a]	Off base	0.12	0.11		0.12	0.11	0.16	−0.16
	On base	0.06	0.07		0.07	0.07	0.09	−0.10
School quality	Off base	0.06		0.08	0.08		0.09	
	On base	0.02		0.05	0.06		0.05	
Child-care spending	Off base							
	On base							
Economic stress scale	Off base							
	On base							

Outcome		RAND BASE-I	Household Composition	Employment	Income and Poverty	Housing	Social	Transportation
Satisfaction								
Satisfaction with base assignment	Off base						0.13	
	On base						0.11	
Satisfaction with Air Force way of life	Off base		−0.04	−0.02			0.13	−0.05
	On base		−0.03	−0.03			0.11	−0.03
Satisfaction with community	Off base						0.21	−0.08
	On base						0.17	−0.06
Career								
Career Intentions	Off base							
	On base							

[a] Asked only of active-duty Airmen.
NOTE: Table contains effect sizes based on only the significant "yes" interactions in the "I" column from Table D.5 (i.e., the model with full controls). Financial stress, employer support, and employer support during deployment are excluded because they were asked only of reserve Airmen.

Appendix E. Detailed Results for Chapter Five, the Caring for People Survey

This appendix provides additional detail from the analyses of the Caring for People Survey. Tables E.1–E.3 report the percentage of survey respondents included in our analyses and descriptive statistics for the survey samples for both active-duty and reserve Airmen. As we did in Appendix D, here we also provide an overview of the modeling strategy and a summary of the overall multilevel model results (see Table E.4). Tables E.5 and E.6 report the effect sizes of the significant coefficients and significant interaction terms from the survey results for the RAND BASE-I and each of the domains.

Table E.1
Percentage of Survey Respondents from the Caring for People Survey Included in the Analysis

Base Area	Respondents (%)	Base Area	Respondents (%)
Altus AFB	97.7	Kirtland AFB	97.8
Arnold AFB	100.0	Laughlin AFB	99.1
Barksdale AFB	94.5	Little Rock AFB	97.0
Beale AFB	92.8	Los Angeles AFB	94.2
Buckley AFB	86.3	Luke AFB	88.0
Cannon AFB	97.5	MacDill AFB	80.8
Columbus AFB	93.2	Malmstrom AFB	97.7
Davis-Monthan AFB	89.8	Maxwell AFB	83.1
Dover AFB	89.8	McConnell AFB	95.5
Dyess AFB	98.5	Minot AFB	98.0
Edwards AFB	91.4	Moody AFB	96.8
Eglin AFB	91.8	Mountain Home AFB	88.0
Eielson AFB	97.7	Nellis AFB	98.0
Ellsworth AFB	98.3	Offutt AFB	98.0
F. E. Warren AFB	97.2	Patrick AFB	85.5
Fairchild AFB	96.6	Peterson AFB	94.5
Goodfellow AFB	96.0	Pope Field AFB	91.0
Grand Forks AFB	97.3	Robins AFB	90.5
Hanscom AFB	91.9	Schriever AFB	96.5
Hill AFB	95.7	Scott AFB	94.1
Holloman AFB	95.3	Seymour Johnson AFB	90.9
Hurlburt Field	97.8	Shaw AFB	95.2
JB Anacostia-Bolling	95.6	Sheppard AFB	94.1
JB Andrews-NAF Washington	92.7	Tinker AFB	92.1
JB Charleston	90.2	Travis AFB	87.9
JB Elmendorf-Richardson	98.5	Tyndall AFB	96.6
JB Langley-Eustis	95.0	U.S. Air Force Academy	97.9
JB Lewis-McChord	91.6	Vance AFB	95.9
JB McGuire-Dix-Lakehurst	87.8	Vandenberg AFB	95.8
JB Pearl Harbor–Hickam	98.5	Whiteman AFB	89.6
JB San Antonio	91.9	Wright-Patterson AFB	92.1
Keesler AFB	88.9	Total	93.5

NOTE: Percentages are based on the 60-mile-boundary definition of *base area*.

Table E.2

Demographic Statistics from the Caring for People Survey: Active Duty Only

Statistic	Overall Mean	On Base	Off Base
Total sample size	33,502	8,935	24,567
Male (%)	75.8	79.1	74.6
Age, in years (standard deviation in parentheses)	32.0 (8.0)	29.6 (8.5)	32.8 (7.7)
Education (%)			
High school or equivalent and below	8.5	14.5	6.0
Some college	57.8	60.5	56.8
College and above	33.7	24.1	37.2
Marital status (%)			
Married	67.7	66.9	68.0
Divorced, separated, or widowed	9.5	4.5	11.4
Never married	22.8	28.6	20.7
Children (%)			
Has any children	50.7	53.5	49.7
Has preschool-age children	27.5	31.5	26.0
Has elementary school–age children	22.9	25.2	22.1
Has secondary school–age children	16.2	14.7	16.7
Officer (%)	23.1	15.3	26.0
Enlisted (%)	76.9	84.7	74.0
Rank (%)			
E1–E4	24.0	44.8	16.5
E5–E6	37.2	29.0	37.2
E7–E8	15.7	10.9	17.4
O1–O3	11.4	5.9	13.4
O4–O6	11.7	9.4	12.5
O7 and above	<1.0	<1.0	<1.0
Years of service (%)			
Less than 4 years	29.4	47.3	22.8
5–10 years	21.2	15.0	23.5
10–20 years	35.6	26.4	38.9
20+ years	13.8	11.3	14.7
Time at base (%)			
Less than 6 months	13.6	16.6	12.6
6–12 months	13.5	19.3	11.4
More than 12 months	72.9	64.1	76.1

Statistic	Overall Mean	On Base	Off Base
Current residence (%)			
On base	23.7	N/A	N/A
Off base	73.3	N/A	N/A
Own home	36.4	49.6	N/A
Rent home	36.7	50.1	N/A
BAH offset: % of mortgage or rent			
More than 100		22.8	
100	N/A	22.8	N/A
75–99	N/A	41.5	N/A
50–74	N/A	10.5	N/A
Less than 50	N/A	2.4	N/A

NOTE: Means are reported.

Table E.3
Demographic Statistics from the Caring for People Survey: Reserve Only

Statistic	Overall Mean
Total sample size	3,849
Male (%)	71.3
Age, in years (standard deviation in parentheses)	41.2 (8.9)
Education (%)	
High school or equivalent and below	N/A
Some college	47.5
College and above	52.6
Marital status (%)	
Married	71.3
Divorced, separated, or widowed	14.6
Never married	14.2
Children (%)	
Has children at home	52.0
Has preschool-age children	18.3
Has elementary school–age children	23.6
Has secondary school–age children	26.1
Employment status (%)	
Full time	69.2
Part time	4.6
Officer (%)	23.5

Statistic	Overall Mean
Enlisted (%)	76.5
Rank (%)	
E1–E4	6.6
E5–E6	34.3
E7–E9	36.0
O1–O3	4.6
O4–O6	18.8
O7 and above	<1.0
Years of service (%)	
Less than 4 years	46.0
5–10 years	30.7
10 to 20 years	21.8
20+ years	1.5
Time at base (%)	
Less than 6 months	40.4
6–12 months	20.8
More than 12 months	38.9

NOTE: Means are reported.

Modeling Strategy

For each RAND BASE-I or domain/outcome combination, we ran three different models: (1) a base model that includes the RAND BASE-I or domain regressed on the outcome (note that each domain is entered independently, without controlling for the other five constituent domains), (2) a model that includes all of the sample characteristics as controls,[54] and (3) a model that includes the controls and an interaction between the RAND BASE-I or domain and an indicator for whether an Airman lives on base. If the interaction is significant, we then ran separate models for Airmen who live in the civilian community (i.e., off base) and those who live in the military community (i.e., on base). Obviously, the interaction model is not applicable to reserve Airmen.

Table E.4 summarizes the results. Outcomes are listed in the rows, while the RAND BASE-I and each of the six domains are listed in the columns. The base model, with no

---

[54] For active-duty Airmen, the control variables include gender, age, education, marital status, age of children (if applicable), rank, years of service, time at current base, and BAH offset (if applicable). Control variables for reserve Airmen are the same except for BAH offset, which is not applicable. Employment status is included only as a control for reserve Airmen. All control variables occur at the individual level. That is, no base-level control variables (e.g., region, population density) are included.

controls, is indicated in the "B" column, the model with control is indicated by a "C," and the model with the interaction is indicated by an "I." In each cell, we indicate whether the association between the RAND BASE-I or domain and the outcome was statistically significant and whether the association was positive or negative. In the cells for the interaction model, the first row indicates whether or not the overall interaction is significant. If it was, we then ran separate models for Airmen who live on base and those who live off base, in the civilian community. Based on those models, a "yes" in the cell indicates that the RAND BASE-I or domain coefficient for living off base is larger than the coefficient for living on base. A "no" in the cell indicates that, although the interaction term is itself significant, the coefficient for living off base (from the separate models for Airmen living off base) is not larger than the coefficient for living on base (again, from the separate model for Airmen living on base).[55]

---

[55] In some cases, the interaction was statistically significant but the RAND BASE-I or domain coefficients for on- and off-base Airmen were in opposite directions. Because this does not support our hypothesis that base-area associations with outcomes are stronger for Airmen who live off base, these cases also receive a "no" in the appropriate cell.

Table E.4
Summary of the Multilevel Model Results from the Caring for People Survey

Outcome		RAND BASE-I			Household Composition			Employment			Income and Poverty			Housing			Social			Transportation		
		B	C	I	B	C	I	B	C	I	B	C	I	B	C	I	B	C	I	B	C	I
Programs and services																						
Base program or service use (total number)	Active duty	N*	N*	—							N*	N*	† Yes							P*	P†	† Yes
	Reserve										N*	N*	† Yes							P*	P*	—
Base service use (children = yes/no)[a]	Active duty				P*	P*	NC					P†	—	N*	N**	—				N†		* Yes
	Reserve				P*		—															—
Base service use (recreation = yes/no)	Active duty	N†	N*	—							N**	N**	—				P*		—	P***	P**	—
	Reserve	N†	N*	—							N**	N***	—				N*	N**	—	P***	P**	—
Base service use (food = yes/no)	Active duty											P†	—				N*	N*	—			
	Reserve			—						—		P†	—									—
Life satisfaction																						
Life satisfaction	Active duty																P*	P*	* Yes	N***	N***	*** Yes
	Reserve			—															—			—
Neighborhood resources																						
Neighborhood rating scale	Active duty	P*	P*	*** Yes			* No	N†		*** No	P*	P*	*** Yes	P**	P**	*** Yes	P*	P*	*** Yes	N*	N*	*** Yes
	Reserve			—			—															
Satisfaction with quality of housing	Active duty	N*	N*	*** No	N*	N†	*** Yes	N*	N*	—	N†	N*	† No	P*		* Yes			—	N**	N†	*** Yes
	Reserve	N*	N*	—	N**	N*	—				N*		—				N*		—		N†	—

[a] footnote

Outcome		RAND BASE-I			Household Composition			Employment			Income and Poverty			Housing			Social			Transportation		
		B	C	I	B	C	I	B	C	I	B	C	I	B	C	I	B	C	I	B	C	I
Satisfaction with health care	Active duty	P*	P*	—						—	P***	P***	—	P*	P*	—	P**	P**	*** Yes	N†	N†	*** Yes
	Reserve			—			—			—			—			—			—			—
Satisfaction with number of civilian friends	Active duty			—			† No			—	P**	P**	* Yes				P*	P†	† Yes	N***	N***	** Yes
	Reserve			—			—			—			—			—		N†	—			—
Leisure satisfaction	Active duty			—			—			—	P**	P**					P***	P***	*** Yes	N***	N***	*** Yes
	Reserve			—		N†	—			—	P*		—			—			—	N*	N***	** Yes
Financial satisfaction	Active duty			—			—			—			—			—			* No	N*		*** Yes
	Reserve			—			—			—			—			—			—	P*	P**	—
Career																						
Remain past obligation or reenlist	Active duty			—	N*	N*	—			—			† Yes	N†		—	P†	P*	† Yes	N**	N***	† Yes
	Reserve	N*	N*	—			—	N*	N*	—			—	N†	N†	—			—			—
Career intention	Active duty			—	N†	N*	—			—		P†	* Yes	N†	N†	—	P*	P*	* Yes	N*	N***	* Yes
	Reserve	N*	N*	—		N*	—	N†	N†	—	N†	N†	—			—			—			—
Impact of career on civilian work[b]	Reserve			—			—			—			—			—			—			—

[a] Model run for parents only. NC = model did not converge.
[b] Asked only of reserve Airmen.

NOTE: B = bivariate association. C = controls included. I = interaction with living on base. N = negative association. P = positive association. † = $p < 0.10$. * = $p < 0.05$. ** = $p < 0.01$. *** = $p < 0.001$. In cells in the I column, the first row indicates significance. If the interaction is significant, separate models are estimated for Airmen who live on versus off base. Yes = coefficient for off base is statistically significantly larger than the coefficient for on base. No = coefficient for off base is not statistically significantly larger than the coefficient for on base or the coefficients are in opposite directions. For active-duty Airmen, the control variables include gender, age, education, marital status, age of children (if applicable), rank, years of service, time at current base, and BAH offset (if applicable). Control variables for reserve Airmen are the same except for BAH offset, which is not applicable. Employment status is included as a control only for reserve Airmen.

Effect Sizes

As we note in Chapter Five, we opted to present results in terms of statistical significance (i.e., the outcomes that showed a statistical association with the RAND BASE-I and its constituent domains). However, statistical significance does not necessarily indicate practical significance. In the tables that follow, we provide effect sizes in order to give the reader a sense of the magnitude of the association between base-area characteristics and Airman outcomes.

Effect sizes for only the significant coefficients from Table E.4 (for the full model with controls) are shown in Table E.5. For continuous variables, effect sizes are calculated by standardizing the entire sample by one whole sample standard deviation (i.e., the standard deviation for the sample as a whole) for both predictor and outcome. For example, the effect size for the social domain's association with life satisfaction among active-duty Airmen is 0.03. A one–standard deviation change on the social domain score results in a 0.03–standard deviation increase in life satisfaction ratings.

Effect sizes for categorical outcomes are calculated by taking the change in probability of the outcome switching from "no" to "yes" if the predictor variable changes by one standard deviation and the outcome had a 0.5 probability of occurring before the change. For example, the effect size for the household composition domain's association with use of child-related base services among active-duty Airmen is 0.01. A one–standard deviation change in household composition domain scores is associated with an increase of using on-base child-related services from 50 percent to 51 percent.

Table E.6 provides effect sizes for only the significant interaction terms from Table E.4. They can be interpreted in the same manner as in Table E.5.

Table E.5

Effect Sizes for Significant Coefficients from the Caring for People Survey Results

Outcome		RAND BASE-I	Household Composition	Employment	Income and Poverty	Housing	Social	Transportation
Programs and services								
Base program or service use (total number)	Active duty				−0.03			0.04
	Reserve	−0.04			−0.05	−0.06		0.05
Base service use (children =yes/no)[a]	Active duty		0.01		0.00			
	Reserve							
Base service use (recreation = yes/no)	Active duty	−0.02			−0.01		−0.01	0.06
	Reserve	−0.02			−0.01		−0.01	0.07
Base service use (food = yes/no)	Active duty				0.02			
	Reserve				0.01			
Life satisfaction								
Life satisfaction	Active duty						0.03	−0.06
	Reserve							
Neighborhood resources								
Neighborhood rating scale	Active duty	0.05			0.05	0.07	0.05	−0.05
	Reserve							
Satisfaction with quality of housing	Active duty		−0.03					−0.03

154